W9-BEN-679

ESKIMO

EASTERN CREE

WOODLAND HUNTERS

MONTAGNAIS

MICMAC

MALECITE
ME.
PASSAMA-
QUODDY
ABENAKI
PENOBSCOT
ALGONQUIN

CHIPPEWA

OTTAWA

VT.
N. PENNACOOK
H.
MOHAWK
ONEIDA
ONONDAGA
CAYUGA
SENECA
MASS. POCOMTUC
WAMPANOAG
PEQUOT
MUNSEE
MOHICAN
CONN.
R. I.
NARRAGANSETT
MONTAUK
N. J.
DELAWARE

ASSINIBOIN

SANTEE
DAKOTA

WIS.

MENOMINEE

FOX

SAUK

WINNEBAGO

POTAWATOMI

MICH.

HURON

TOBACCO
NATION

NEUTRALS

ERIE

IROQUOIANS

N. Y.

PA.

Connecticut R.

FARMERS

KICKAPOO

IOWA

ILL.

MIAMI

OHIO

NORTH

MO.

OSAGE

MISSOURI

ILLINOIS

IND.

SHAWNEE

KY.

HONIASONT

MOSOPELEA

MONETON

W. VA.

VA.

MONACAN

SAPONI

PAMUNKEY

TUTELO

MATTAPONI

ENO

NOTTOWAY

POWHATAN

MD.

NANTICOKE

DEL.

SUSQUEHANNA

EAST

CHEROKEE

N. C.

PAMLICO

TUSCARORA

KASKINAMPO

YUCHI

CHERAW

CATAWBA

S. C.

WATEREE

WACCAMAW

TENN.

SOUTH

UPPER
CREEKS

EAST

SANTEE

CUSABO

YAMASI

Mississippi R.

ARK.

QUAPAW

HOUMA

CHICKASAW

MISS.

CHOCTAW

KOASATI

ALA.

LOWER CREEKS

HITCHITI

GA.

GUALE

CADDO

TUNICA

YAZOO

KOROA

TAENSA

LA.

NATCHEZ

BILOXI

ALIBAMU

APALACHEE

TAKARA

CHITIMACHA

TIMUCUA

AIS

CALUSA

FLA.

TEKESTA

INDIAN TRIBES—1650

Southwest
High Plains
Western Farmers
Northeast
Southeast
Woodland Hunters
Northwest Coast
Plateau
Great Basin
California

Illustrated with color photographs, contemporary paintings, prints, and specially commissioned paintings by André Durenceau

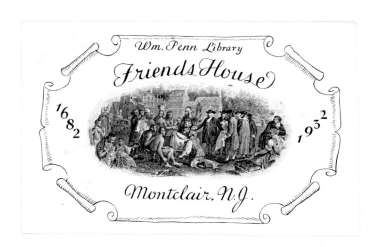

OLIVER LA FARGE

THE AMERICAN INDIAN

Special Edition for Young Readers

GOLDEN PRESS NEW YORK

The author and publishers would like to express their deep gratitude to all who have given time and help, and particularly to the following institutions and individuals. American Museum of Natural History—R. E. Logan. Arizona State Museum—E. B. Sayles. Museum of the American Indian/Heye Foundation—Dr. F. J. Dockstader, C. Guadagno. Museum of Modern Art—B. Karpel. Peabody Museum of Archaeology and Ethnology—Mrs. K. B. Edsall. New York Public Library—Mr. Stark. New York State Museum—Dr. W. N. Fenton. Philbrook Art Center—Mrs. J. Snodgrass. Smithsonian Institution: Bureau of American Ethnology—Dr. F. H. H. Roberts, Jr., Dr. W. C. Sturtevant, Mrs. M. C. Blaker; U. S. National Museum—Dr. F. M. Setzler, R. A. Elder. University of New Mexico—Dr. F. C. Hibben, Dr. M. Lambert. Mrs. Fred Block. Miss Laura Gilpin, Mr. Barney Burstein, Col. L. H. Frohman.

The source of each illustration, the page it appears on, and when applicable, its position on the page are given below. The following abbreviations are used: l=left; r=right; t=top; b=bottom; c=center. The pictures and caption material on pages 187, 188 are taken from The Peyote Ritual by Monroe Tsa Toke, © 1957 by Mrs. Leslie Van Ness Denman. They are used here through the courtesy of the members of the Denman family. Maps on pages 8, 24, 38, 52, 66, 86, 120, 144, 162, 194 by Elmer Smith. Cover and jacket painting by Ned E. Seidler.

CHUCK ABBOTT/RAPHO GUILLUMETTE—90; 100.
ANSEL ADAMS—Acoma Pueblo 7.
RALPH ALTMAN—Shoshone robe 150.
AMERICAN MUSEUM OF NATURAL HISTORY—10t; bowls 13tl, tc; shaman 24; 26b; 68t; 71t; 75c; 80; 121b; 124; 125b; 138b; 144b; 158; 162tl; 163b; 167; baskets 170; 174tl; 175tr; 180t; 184; 185b; 192b.
ARIZONA STATE MUSEUM—goat, pot 12; bowls 13tr, cr, c, cl, lower l; jar 13; 18b; 88b; 91b; 93; 97tl; baskets 115.
ASHMOLEAN MUSEUM, OXFORD—cloak 62 (photo courtesy Smithsonian Institution).
BETHLEHEM STEEL COMPANY, INC.—198.
DR. BLOCK COLOR PRODUCTIONS, INC.—color photographs on pages 2tr, tl, br; 3tl; 8t; 9tr; 20c—upper and lower; 21 upper c; 22c; 23tc; 30b; 52b; 149t; 150c; 152 except br; 156tr; 157 except tr; 168t; cl; 169bl; 170tr; cl; 171 except t; 173t; 174 bl, cr, br; 175br; 176; 177cr, b; 178tl; 179tr, cr, cl, br; 180tl; 207bl; 208tr; 214br; 215tl, tc, bl.

BRITISH MUSEUM—27t.
IN THE BROOKLYN MUSEUM COLLECTION—172b.
BARNEY BURSTEIN—color photographs on pages 22tl, tr, bl; 23b; 25bl, br; 32; 33t; 36t; 65t; 69; 76b; 78t; 82t; 126bl; 170b; 175l; 162b.
CANADIAN NATIONAL RAILWAYS—totem poles 180-1 (except 1st and 3rd from left), 169.
DR. CHAPMAN—Kachina doll 86.
CHICAGO NATURAL HIST. MUSEUM 175b.
CITY ART MUSEUM OF ST. LOUIS 19b; 28.
MEMBERS OF THE DENMAN FAMILY 187; 188.
DENVER ART MUSEUM—30b; coat 58; jar 89; baskets 92, 150c, 151tr, 157cr, b; adze 169; hat 170; headdress 176; bracelet 179; adze 181; basket 207; mask 208.
DEXTER PRESS—29t; women 35; 108t; horseman 117; 205.
MRS. CHARLES DIETRICH—86b; 101b; 103b; 108c; 113b; 115t; 138; 208b.
HENRY FRANCIS DUPONT WINTERTHUR MUSEUM—33.
LOUIS H. FROHMAN—color photographs on pages 4; 35tr; 68b; 73b; 76t; 77; 81b; 84; 110tl, bl; 111br; 121t; 124-5; 131.
GILCREASE INSTITUTE, TULSA, OKLA.—37t; 140; 141t; 142-3.
LAURA GILPIN—color photographs on pages 6; 86c, b; 94; 96-7 except 97tl; 98; 99; 101; 102-3 except 103tl; 104; 108c, b; 109b; 195b; 200; 203tr; 204; 207br; 208tl, b; 210t. Black and white photograph 103c.
C. GUADAGNO—color photographs 187, 188.
A. C. HECTOR—74; wickeyup 114.
INDIAN ARTS FUND—96b; 97c; 98 (lower picture): necklace far right, bracelet lower right, crescent earrings; 99 (upper picture) necklaces, center bracelet; 99 (lower picture): center belt buckle. 109b except red upper l, blue upper r, red and white bottom; 214br.
KENNEDY GALLERIES, INC.—Catlin paintings 120, 129, 133, 134, 137.
LABORATORY OF ANTHROPOLOGY—96tl, cr; 109b red upper l, blue upper r, red and white bottom; 110c; 111c; 199tl; 99b.
BEN LEWIS—203bl, br.
LIBRARY OF CONGRESS—Hunting Seminoles 35; 64; 65b.
LOS ANGELES COUNTY MUSEUM—basket 149t; 156tr; Mission basket, Shasta hat 157; Yakatut basket 170.
RAY MANLEY—color photographs 12; 91; 93; baskets 115; 195t.
PIERRE MARTINOT—Mayan temple 19.
MERCALDO ARCHIVES—160b.
MESA VERDE NAT'L PARK MUSEUM—17t.
METROPOLITAN MUSEUM OF ART, ROGERS FUND, 1907—146-7.
HOLMES I. METTEE STUDIO—160t; 164.
MONTANA HISTORICAL SOCIETY—152-3.
DAVID MUENCH—Acoma Pueblo 18.
JOSEPH MUENCH—color photographs on pages 15; 87; 88-9; 145; 159b.
MUSEUM OF THE AMERICAN INDIAN/HEYE FOUNDATION — moccasins, quiver, drum, rattle 2; tomahawk, jar, ivory figure, effigy figure, sash, bag 3; pipe, ram 9; 12t; pot, mask, diorite bowl 20; figure, frog, axe, basket 21; pottery 22cl, c, br; gorgets 22t; pot 25; 29b; 34b; mask 37; mask 38; 39tr, tc, tl; basket 42; earrings, leggings 43; 45r; pipes 46; vest, boxes 52; 54c, b; 58tr, c, b; 58; 59; 79b; 83b; 85b; shirt 114; leggings 115; headdress 116; shield 120; 125tr, cr; 126 except bl; moccasins, ornament, robe 127; headdresses 130; bags 134; shield, drum, rattle 136; hat, lower basket 149; dress, baby carrier 150; drum 151; hat 155; baskets 156tl, cl, c, cr; 157tr; 161br, bl; mortar, dish, beaver 168; headdress, mortar 169; 172t; 174tr; staff, rattle 177; 179tl; 185t; fan 186; 192t; 193; basket 194; box, ladle, head, bag, jar, tomahawk 214; thunderbird, pot, sash 215.
MUSEUM OF NAVAHO CEREMONIAL ART—106-7; 112; 113tl; 113tr.
MUSEUM OF NEW MEXICO—Ma Pe Wi:

"Winnowing Grain" 2; 97tr; ring 99t.
MUSEUM OF NORTHERN ARIZONA—murals 14, 212. (Photos by Parker Hamilton.)
NATIONAL ARCHIVES—Sitting Bull 143.
NEW-YORK HISTORICAL SOCIETY—27b; 48t; 49.
NEW YORK PUBLIC LIBRARY—Seminole 35; 84t; 110tl, tr, br; 111tl, br. Bodmer paintings 4, 66, 68b; 73b; 76t, 77, 78b, 81, 84b, 121t, 124-5, 131t.
NEW YORK STATE MUSEUM—comb 2; coat and bag 37; cradle 38; pot, sash, belts 42; moccasins, belt 43; masks 44-5 except r; 47; 48b; belt 51; fan 214; rattle 215.
BETTY O'CONNOR—105; 109t; 118; 119b.
OHIO HISTORICAL SOCIETY—claw 2; figure 8; hand 20; pipe 215.
PEABODY MUSEUM OF ARCHAEOLOGY AND ETHNOLOGY (HARVARD)—earrings 2; pot 9; 22tl, tr, bl; 23b; 25t, b; 26; 28b; 36t; 52b; 65t; 69; 76b; 126bl; basket 157c; 162b; 166; 170b; clan hat 175; McKenney & Hall portraits: 32, 78, 82.
PENNSYLVANIA HIST. SOCIETY—83.
PHILADELPHIA MUSEUM OF ART—whale 144.
PHILBROOK ART CENTER—67; 102; 119t; 129t; 131b; 132t; 135; 209br.
PORTLAND (ORE.) ART MUSEUM/RASMUSSEN COLLECTION—headdress 3; 174bl; 176b; blanket 178; 179cl.
BERNARD POWELL—Micmap tepee 57.
PROVINCIAL MUSEUM, VICTORIA, BRITISH COLUMBIA—slate carving 168; 171cl, cr; 174br; crest model 176; totem poles 180 (1st and 3rd from left); 183t; mask 215t.
RHODE ISLAND SCHOOL OF DESIGN—63b.
ROCHESTER MUSEUM OF ARTS AND SCIENCES—46t; wood carving 209.
ROYAL ONTARIO MUSEUM (CANADA)—75b; 136l; 137t; 152t; 171t.
ROBERT STOLPER—173t.
SOUTHWEST MUSEUM—basket 151tl.
SMITHSONIAN INSTITUTION (BUREAU OF AMERICAN ETHNOLOGY)—15b; 18c; 24b; 27c; Choctaw, chiki 35 (Sturtevant); 36b; 39b; 51b; 62t; lodge 73; village 75; 82-3; 95; 111tr; Geronimo 116; 117tl, bl; 127t; cl; 128; necklace 129; War Eagle, Red Cloud 130; 133; 137br; 148; 153; 159t; peyote, Wovoka 186; 189; 190; 191 (Fenton); 197b. (U.S. NATIONAL MUSEUM)—9b; prayer stick 79; pouches, beadwork 114; 116l; dishes 169; 173b; mask 215cl; Catlin paintings 30, 31, 34, 72, 73, 79, 85, 127tr, 133, 139, 161.
PANSY STOCKTON—104tr, tc, bc.
TAYLOR MUSEUM OF THE COLORADO SPRINGS FINE ARTS CENTER—151tc.
TULANE UNIVERSITY—8b; 14t; 103tl.
RUTH UNDERHILL—temple 19c from Red Man's America.
UNIVERSITY OF CALIFORNIA PRESS—hut 149 from California Indians; cradle 168, mask 178 Frank Smith Collection, Vancouver; from Art of the Northwest Coast Indians, by Bruce Inverarity.
UNIVERSITY OF COLORADO 11t; 174c.
UNIVERSITY MUSEUM, UNIVERSITY OF PENNSYLVANIA—deer's head 21.
UNIVERSITY OF NEW MEXICO—murals 3, 15.
UNIVERSITY OF OKLAHOMA PRESS—160t; 164t courtesy of the Walters Art Gallery, Baltimore, © 1951 by the University of Oklahoma Press, Norman; 142b West of Alfred Jacob Miller © 1951 Univ. of Okla. Press—Walters Art Gallery.
U.S. DEPARTMENT OF THE INTERIOR—194b; 196; Paul Jones, Chee Dodge 199; 201; 202-3; 206tl, tr; 207t; 210-11.
WASHINGTON STATE MUSEUM—bag, belt 151; 163t; 171b; fish emblem 176; box 177; shirt 179cr; robe 179br.

CONTENTS

The Adena Figure: a stone pipe from Ohio of 1,000 years ago

They Discovered America

Hopi men set forth to look for rattlesnakes. The Snake Ceremony is an ancient religious rite and the men are wearing the same sort of garment that their ancestors wore centuries ago. This photograph is one of a number of Snake Ceremony pictures that were taken about 1910

Most of the people who were to become Indians crossed into the New World from Siberia. They came over slowly, in small groups, over a period of fifteen thousand years or more. Here and there, from Canada to central Mexico, archaeologists have found traces of these early settlers. They have found the remains of their campfires, bones of the animals they hunted, and tools of flint, bone, and wood.

The tip of Siberia was a bleak and isolated region, occupied by tribes who had been pushed there from more favored lands and were too weak to force their way back. Deserts, vast distances, and mountain ranges cut the people off, insulated them from the civilizing developments that were going on elsewhere. The news of a discovery or invention made in one of the centers of civilization—in China, India, Asia Minor, or around the Mediterranean—spread widely in a thousand years or so, but it might never reach the inhabitants of Siberia at all. Many of the settlers, moreover, made the crossing into America before any of the discoveries that changed the history of the Old World had been made; the latest finds, tested by what is called the radiocarbon method, reveal that men had reached New Mexico and Texas 20,000 years ago, long before mankind anywhere had emerged from the Old Stone Age. So remote an area is Siberia, however, that even those who crossed at a later date would not have known about the new ideas.

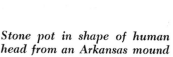

A 17th century pipe from Rhode Island of a type once widespread in eastern North America

Stone pot in shape of human head from an Arkansas mound

Stone mountain sheep mortar of the Hohokam culture of Arizona

From time to time, during thousands of years, groups of people crossed over into the New World. They were different physically, had different ways and customs, spoke different languages. In their new homes, they changed yet more, sometimes becoming more alike through intermarriage and the exchange of ideas, sometimes more different. There is thus no such thing as "an Indian culture," nor is there such a thing as "an Indian language," any more than there is "a European language."

In time the various families of settlers moved throughout and populated North and South America, and became yet more remote from the Old World. Here, in an unfamiliar land, they had to make their own discoveries. The Old World had livestock and beasts of burden; there were camels, horses, elephants in Asia, cattle, sheep, goats, and pigs, as well as chickens, ducks, and geese. The early Americans learned to raise and tame turkeys, but birds cannot be used to do work. Llamas, small animals related to camels and capable of carrying a load of about fifty pounds, were domesticated and put to work in Ecuador and Peru. But the big animals of North America, like the elephants in Africa, could not be tamed.

So also, in the Old World there were many kinds of grain such as wheat, rye, oats, barley, and millet that could be planted by scattering the seeds in fertile ground. In the New World there was only one, maize, which most of us know as corn. Anyone who

has ever planted corn knows that it cannot be sown broadcast; each grain must be set in a hole. It required a lot of experimenting and centuries of time to develop from the original, wild grass a plant that would yield a decent crop.

Farming began and spread through the middle part of the Americas from Peru to central Mexico. Beans may have been cultivated as early as the first corn, and in time a variety of other plants were developed, such as pumpkins, squashes, tobacco, potatoes, sweet potatoes, chocolate, tomatoes, peanuts, and many others that are now part of the world's diet. Cotton is the only plant that was developed both in the Old World and the New.

Slowly, centers of civilization grew up, and the Americas began to repeat the history of the Old World. The early civilizations whose names are best

Some of the Mound Builders built "effigy mounds" in the shape of various birds and animals. One of the best known of these mounds is the Great Serpent Mound in southern Ohio. Measured along its curves, this mound from head to tail is approximately 1,400 feet in length

9

Pueblo burial of about A.D. 1000. Modern Southwestern designs as shown on pages 108-110 continue the tradition of the designs that decorate this fine, ancient cotton robe

known to us are the Incas, the Toltecs, and the Mayas. These had cities, handsome architecture, fine art, forms of writing, mathematics, and astronomy. The people still used stone tools, although they were not what we think of as "Stone Age" people. They were on the edge of the change to metals. Gold, silver, and copper were worked, but mostly for ornaments.

In the Old World, barbarians time and again attacked the centers of civilization, conquered them, became civilized themselves, and carried on the line of progress. The same thing happened in the Americas. Notably, barbarous people speaking a language of the Uto-Aztecan family came down from the north to invade the cities of central Mexico. There they conquered the ancient Toltecs, acquired their civilization, and became the Aztecs.

The influence of the civilized centers constantly spread outward, as it did in the Old World. This civilizing influence spread north into what is now the United States through two principal areas: the Southeast and the Southwest.

Indian life as it probably was at the beginning of the true Pueblo period is shown below

By the Southwest is meant Arizona and New Mexico and narrow strips of neighboring territory, especially in northern Mexico, southern Colorado, and Utah. A thousand miles of harsh desert and mountain country lay between this area and the cities to the south, but indirect trade was carried on between the Southwesterners and the central Mexicans. Goods passed from tribe to tribe in a long series of exchanges. The civilized people got turquoise from the north; the northerners received, among other things, parrot feathers and seeds. More important, ideas were passed along with the goods—the *idea* of farming, of weaving, of making pottery, of putting on masks so as to represent sacred beings.

A good deal more is known about the very early history of the Southwest than about other parts of

Sandals, woven 1,500 years ago from yucca fibers by the Basketmakers, are shown above

Wherever conditions allowed in the Southwest, the people farmed extensively, beginning with native beans and corn from the south. Many of them learned to irrigate; others became expert dry farmers.

The earliest known farmers in North America, part of the longest continuous cultural line that archaeologists can trace, were the people of what is called the "Cochise culture" of southern Arizona and New Mexico. They were raising a primitive form of corn three thousand years ago. From the Cochise, in the course of a thousand years or so, derived the Mogollon and Hohokam cultures; and the Hohokam people, it is believed, were ancestors of the modern Pimans of southern Arizona.

The most famous of the Southwestern cultures is the Pueblo, not only because of the spectacular ruins of these people, but because the culture is so well continued by their modern descendants.

The Pueblos came into being when a new people, with round heads, entered the country along the Colorado and Utah border and intermingled with the earlier, long-headed inhabitants, who belonged to the ancient Basketmaker culture. They combined to form one people, and later spread southward. Other groups of farmers adopted the Pueblo culture and contributed to it, so that in prehistoric times, as today, the Pueblo Indians consisted of many tribes speaking several languages.

the country, for two reasons. For many thousands of years the Southwest has been fairly dry, although not as arid as it is now. In dry country, the remains that people leave behind them last much longer; and in dry country, where vegetation is sparse, it is easy for archaeologists to spot the right places to dig. Furthermore, many of the tribes living in the Southwest today are direct descendants of tribes that lived there more than a thousand years ago. Oraibi, a Hopi village, has been continuously inhabited since A.D. 1100. The modern Indians retain the languages and a great many of the ways of their ancestors, as well as a knowledge of the ancient tribal traditions.

Pottery mountain goat made by the ancient Hohokam people of southern Arizona. These people dropped from sight around 1400 but many Indians who still farm parts of southern Arizona may be descended from them

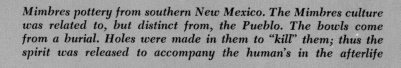

Mimbres pottery from southern New Mexico. The Mimbres culture was related to, but distinct from, the Pueblo. The bowls come from a burial. Holes were made in them to "kill" them; thus the spirit was released to accompany the human's in the afterlife

Black-on-white jar of the Hohokam culture

13

Hopi Snake Society men leaving their kiva at Oraibi, another of the unique 1910 photographs; since then, no photography of this ceremony has been permitted

They built villages of stone houses cemented with *adobe*, a local clay. In each village were one or more *kivas*, which were men's clubs and also centers of religious ceremonial. Kivas were built partly or entirely underground and were entered through a hole in the roof. Their basic form derived from an ancient type of "pit house," built by such earlier people as the Basketmakers. Later, kivas were elaborated beyond any resemblance to those early structures, and some of them were decorated with handsome murals depicting sacred subjects.

Most hills in the Southwest are of the kind called *mesas*, having flat tops and very steep, rock sides. Sections of these sides scale off, leaving deep ledges overhung by the upper part of the cliff. Two thousand or more years ago, the Southwestern Indians often built their houses on these ledges for shelter from the weather. Later they built their towns on them, although often that meant the women had to climb up and down the cliffs every day to carry water, and all the crops or other food had to be dragged or carried up. Such towns are called cliff dwellings.

Mural decorations from a prehistoric Hopi kiva, showing stylized sacred figures and symbols

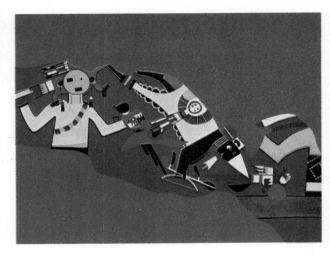

Betata Kin, a late 13th century cliff dwelling in north-eastern Arizona. In the foreground is a kiva like the one the Hopi men are leaving on the page opposite

Section of a kiva mural at Pottery Mound, a late Pueblo ruin in central New Mexico. This ruin is at present being dug by the staff of the University of New Mexico

Painting of a ceremony in a Hopi kiva, consecrating prayer plumes to the gods of rain. The altar, in the middle, is made by grinding colored earth and rocks, then arranging them on the ground in a design that varies with the ceremony being held

It was probably for defense as well as shelter that the Pueblos built their towns in such places. Between A.D. 1000 and 1200, savage tribes began drifting into the Southwest, the ancestors of the Navahos and Apaches who had broken off from tribes settled in northern Canada and Alaska. The invaders were primitive and poor, but they had an Arctic-type bow, originally of Asian origin, that was stronger than any bow known in the Southwest. This gave them a military advantage. The newcomers did not make regular war upon the Pueblo people; they traded with them, they learned from them, they stole from them, and from time to time they raided them. However, they were enough of a nuisance to make the Pueblos want to have their settlements strong and defensible.

Later, when the Pueblos moved out of the section in which their culture first developed, they built their towns on high places, or arranged them so that the houses themselves formed a defensive wall.

Pueblo culture was essentially peaceful and democratic. Few indications of fighting have been found, in spite of the trouble these semi-civilized people must have had with nomadic, primitive bands. In ancient times the Pueblos were governed by a theocracy—that

Black and white jar found in a kiva in Mesa Verde

is, by their priests and religious officials—but the governors' power derived from the consent of the governed. The Pueblo culture shows very few signs of the elaborate, special burials of a few individuals that occur where there is much distinction of rank, nor are there special houses finer than others. The modern Pueblo Indians, too, are peaceful and democratic. The labor they put into building their kivas is a community effort, undertaken voluntarily.

The culture of the Southwest never spread far beyond Arizona, New Mexico, and the southernmost

Daily life at Mesa Verde during the Classic Period, A.D. 1050-1300. The kiva in the foreground and the buildings are well built and, due to their position on the cliff face, easily defended. However, the men toiling uphill with a deer are evidence that while these cliff dwellings are picturesque, they must have been mighty inconvenient

Acoma Pueblo (above) was inhabited when the Spaniards arrived in the Southwest in 1540, and has been lived in ever since. Pueblo Bonito (below), another ancient pueblo, was probably settled by people from Mesa Verde

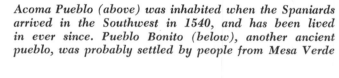

Reconstruction of Pueblo Bonito viewed from its walled front side

parts of Colorado and Utah. Beyond, in most directions, were high mountains or deserts which could not be farmed with primitive equipment. To the east lay the High Plains, which were also unsuitable for primitive farming. As we are now learning, they are not suited to modern farming either.

The other area through which Mexican influence came into the United States, the Southeast, was utterly different. We do not as yet know the Southeastern story in as great detail as we do the Southwestern, nor can we carry it as far back. What we do know is that about a thousand years ago a remarkable culture had spread from the Gulf Coast up the Mississippi Valley almost to the Great Lakes. It, too, was based on farming. It is called the "Mound Builder" culture, because the people went in heavily for building mounds.

Direct Mexican influence can clearly be seen in this region. Trait after trait, from the weaving of feather cloaks to a highly organized aristocracy, came from the great cities of Mexico. A striking evidence of this influence is the very matter of mounds.

The Toltecs, Aztecs, and Mayas built flat-topped pyramids on which they placed their temples and sometimes their palaces. They built with stone, mortar, and a kind of concrete. Pyramids and buildings were arranged in impressive groups that served

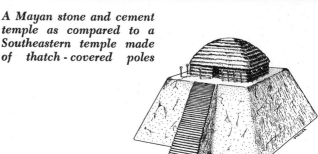

A Mayan stone and cement temple as compared to a Southeastern temple made of thatch-covered poles

as religious and civic centers for the humble farmers who lived roundabout. The people along the Mississippi Valley built similar centers, although in a cruder style. The mounds were made of rubble covered with earth, the temples and other buildings of wood and thatch. Nonetheless, the form was the same.

A Mississippi burial mound being excavated, part of a huge panorama painted in 1850

A Southeastern pot in the shape of a head. The scratches represent tattooing

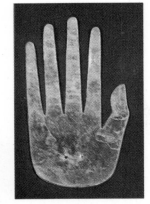

Symbol of human hand made of thin mica by Ohio Mound Builders

Wooden mask of deer's head from Oklahoma. The eyes and mouth are pieces of shell

North of the Ohio River, the people developed a mound pattern of their own, building what are called "effigy mounds." These are figures of birds or animals, made of modeled earth, often placed on top of ordinary mounds.

The people lived in fairly permanent villages and towns, their houses usually made with wattled walls and roofs either thatched or covered with mats. They farmed extensively. They also developed the finest art, especially in modeling and carving, that ever existed among the North American Indians.

The largest mound built by the Mound Builders is the Cahokia Mound in Illinois, which is 1,100 feet long by 700 feet wide and 100 feet high. Others, however, are almost equally imposing. Construction of this kind, without any machinery at all, without even wheelbarrows, calls for a staggering number of man-hours. It requires two conditions. The first is a food supply so plentiful that the people can lay in all they need to eat and still have abundant time for other work; the second is the authority to hold them at hard labor.

The Pueblo Indians of the Southwest put in a lot of work to build their kivas, as we would build a town hall or a church—something that every man would use frequently. The Southeasterners, on the other hand, built enormous structures that the common man used only occasionally. It is certain that over the laboring people there was an aristocracy of great power. It is not surprising, then, that in this culture we find elaborate tombs of rulers, some of whom were so great that servants or slaves were killed and buried with them. In the existence of a ruling upper class, perhaps of kings, can be seen another influence from Mexico.

The Mississippi Valley, with its relatively civilized settlements and its rich booty, was very tempting to the more primitive tribes that surrounded it. It was bound to be invaded, and it seems to have been

Bowl shaped as crested wood duck. It is carved from diorite, a hard stone

completely overrun a few centuries before the white men came there. In the south, the invaders took over a good deal of the old civilization but did not come up to the level of the great period; in the country of the effigy mound people, to the north, the new occupants were distinctly primitive.

One nation, the Natchez, which survived at the time of the arrival of the white men, may well have descended directly from the older people. Its center was a famous structure, the great Emerald Mound, in Mississippi. Alone among all the historic North American Indian tribes and nations, the Natchez had an absolute monarch. The king, called "The Sun," was so sacred that he could not defile himself by setting his foot to the ground, and so was carried about on a litter. He wore a feather crown and an elaborate feather cloak. Volunteers became his servants, and of their own accord had themselves killed when The Sun died, so that they might accompany him in the afterlife. The Sun had absolute power over his people.

The Natchez were divided into two halves, the aristocracy and the common people. The aristocracy was subdivided into three classes: Suns, or royalty; Nobles; and Honorables. The common people were lumped together in a single group and called Stinkers.

The catch to this was that the common people could marry as they pleased, but the aristocrats were allowed to marry only Stinkers. When a male aristocrat married a common woman, his children were rated one level lower than himself, so that the children of a male Noble became Honorables, and those of a male Honorable became ordinary Stinkers. When a female aristocrat married a male Stinker, her children inherited her rank. Thus even The Sun himself was half Stinker on his father's side, his rank having come to him through his mother.

The advanced culture of the Southwest was confined by the geography of the country surrounding

Southeastern jar in form of seated figure

Arkansas bowl in shape of frog. This is one of many animal forms used by Southeastern Indians

Wooden head of young deer or doe from Key Marco, Florida

Well-preserved axe and basket from the Ozark Mountains. They are the work of the forerunners of the Choctaw and the Chickasaw Indian tribes

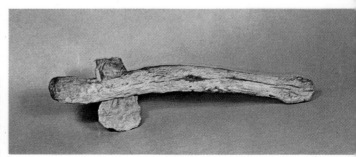

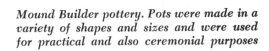

Mound Builder pottery. Pots were made in a variety of shapes and sizes and were used for practical and also ceremonial purposes

Catawba bowl. The Catawbas still make fine pottery in the traditional style

Arkansas jar. The design was painted, the jar fired, then the paint scraped off. Thus the design came out the same color as the clay before firing

Arkansas water bottle of a type that was used when the Spanish arrived in America

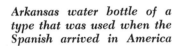

Painted pottery bowl from Arkansas

Colorful, decorated pottery of the Mound Builders, found at Moundsville, Alabama

Southeastern Mound Builder carved shell gorgets. These were worn at the throat or just below it, suspended from a string. Many of the decorations used by the South-easterners on their gorgets show a strong Mexican influence, Aztec or possibly Mayan

it, but fertile land lay east, west, and north of the Southeast-Mississippi Valley culture. The art of farming spread out from the center as far as conditions made it possible to raise crops. It reached into Canada, westward to the line beyond which rainfall averages less than twenty inches a year, and eastward to the Atlantic Coast. To varying degrees, the outlying tribes adopted some of the arts of the advanced culture, and some of its social organization.

Wherever farming was carried on, the Indians tended to stay put. The farmers moved when they were forced to, or, as most of them used no fertilizer, when the fields became poor. A family with a planted field is not going to walk off and leave it; a family with a ton or so of grain stored up is not going to lug it around just for fun. However, nowhere in the United States did people rely solely on farming. The population of the country before the white men came was not over a million. There was plenty of room, and the hunting and fishing were wonderful. Naturally, farming was balanced by the pursuit of fish and game. The proportion of farming to hunting and fishing differed from region to region and from tribe to tribe. Environment had much to do with determining this proportion, as had the degree of culture that a specific tribe had attained.

Most Americans think that for a long time, Indians had been just as they were when the white men found them. This idea is mistaken. The Indians were in the middle of the same process of change that covered so large a part of the Old World. Civilization

was spreading. It advanced, fell back, advanced again, always gaining ground with each forward spurt. North America was at much the same level of advancement as Europe three thousand years earlier. In it burned a small flame which in time could have become a great light. Then the white men landed, wave on wave, with the savage strength that came from steel, gunpowder, and horses, and that small but promising flame was put out forever.

An 18th century Natchez Indian wearing a feather cloak. This cloak is similar to those worn in prehistoric times

A shaman, dancing

The Kings of the South

A dwelling of the Seminoles of Florida, sketched in the 1880's. A mortar and pestle and iron axe lie beside it

The exploration of North America began in the sixteenth century with Spanish expeditions along the Gulf Coast from Florida to Texas, and inland into Georgia and Tennessee. A few of the tribes found by the Spanish and, later, by French and English explorers may have been descended from the ancient Mound Builders. Most were descended from more barbarous peoples who had overrun most of the Mound Builder country and partly destroyed that culture, partly absorbed it and carried it on. Among these were tribes that became famous in American history—the Creeks, Chickasaws, Choctaws, Cherokees, and Seminoles. Others of this group, such as the Natchez in Mississippi, the Timucuas of Florida, the Tunicas on the border of Texas, the Houmas and Chitimachas in southern Louisiana, the Catawbas in South Carolina, gradually faded away and today are extinct, or survive only as feeble remnants.

These Southeastern Indians were quite unlike the commonly accepted ideas of how Indians look and live. They knew nothing of war bonnets, of the dome-shaped wigwams of the New England Indians, or

Illinois and Atakapa Indians sketched at New Orleans in 1735 with a Fox captive and a small Negro boy. The boxes are labeled (left to right) sowbelly, suet, and bear's grease

of the conical skin tents we call tepees. They were farming people, and they lived near their farmlands in large settlements that the early colonists and explorers called towns. The heart of each town was a council house and public square. The houses were solidly built, of wood, bark, thatch, and reeds. In the northern and mountain sections, they were walled; in the extreme south, where the climate was milder, they often had no walls at all.

In warm weather, the people wore almost no clothes. Men put on a breechclout, women draped a bit of skirt around their middles. When it turned cool, they wrapped robes around themselves, and the men sometimes wore leggings of buckskin. Women usually wore their hair long. Frequently the men shaved their heads, or plucked the hairs, in different patterns. When they did this, they always left the "scalp lock." Any man worth his salt was a warrior, and his scalp lock was a challenge to enemies to try to collect his scalp.

The men decorated their bodies with tattooing, or "scratching." When a boy was first given a name, he

While dating only from about 1920, this pot is in the traditional style of Catawba pottery

Basketry made by Chitimacha Indians of Louisiana

25

TEMPLE des Sauvages, construit de Poteaux en terre, revêtu de ... natte de Cannes, et couvert de même ... terminé par trois ... de Bois, de 5. pieds ... de long 1s. pouces ... et sp d'épaisseur, ... matachez et sou ... grossierement les ... s. pyramides su ... natte garnie de ... cañes pointü ... garentir, que ... lon ne puisse ... monter au ... Figures qui rep ... resente de ... d'Indes par 1s ... corps et ... la quelle la ... teste rep ... esente celle ... de l'Aigle ... ce qui nous a ... parû de ... plus approchan

CABANE du Chef de porgouen garnie de Bauge ou marli de terre, couverte aussy ... de natte.

n° Le temple a 22.piedz de ... longueur et 1s pieds de large ... il de Sepulture au ... Chefs de la Nations ... Toutes les Caban ... des Sauvages sont de ... pareille construct ... ion, etants toutes ... Rondes, celle cy ... a 1s.piedst de ... diametre.

Levez et dessinez au Village des Colas-Pissas le quinze avril de la pre annee. Redigez ala nouvelle Orleans le Vingt et deux Juin 1732.

Echelle de six huit Pieds

A temple and a dwelling of the Acolapissa Indians of southern Louisiana are shown in this sketch dated 1732

was scratched. When he became an apprentice warrior, he was named and scratched again, and when he had proved himself by bringing back an enemy scalp, or perhaps the whole head or an arm or a leg, he received a final name and more tattoo marks.

The Southeasterners farmed on a large scale. In the spring the men and women prepared the ground and planted, and the songs ran from field to field. Through the growing season the women did most of the work, for the fields belonged to them, but in the fall men and women harvested together.

When roasting ears were ready for eating, some of the tribes held a great ceremony, the "Green Corn Ceremony." Until this was held, no corn could be eaten, no matter how hungry a person might be. The ceremony was accompanied by elaborate ritual. Old pottery was broken, the fires were put out, the towns were cleaned. Then a new fire was kindled in the temple, and carried to all the hearths. Everyone feasted and a fine, fresh, new year started.

This ceremony, with its ritual theme of ending the old and starting anew, strongly suggests similar,

The wife of a mid-16th century Timucua chief is carried to an important ceremony

but more elaborate, rites practiced in Mexico. There, every fifty-two years, at the close of the sacred period or cycle that the Aztecs thought of somewhat as we think of a century, there took place a great destroying of old things and a cleaning and general preparation for a fresh start. All fires were quenched and new fires laid—something with much more meaning to those people than to us, since, without matches or flint and steel, lighting fires was a tedious job.

The Aztecs had a system of writing and an elaborate calendar, and so were able to keep track of fifty-two-year cycles. The people of the Southeast had no writing. It would be natural for them, if they had heard of the Mexican ceremony, to hold theirs annually and to tie it to an important, good event such as the ripening of the corn.

We tend to think of the famous tribes as organized units. They were not. All the Creeks, for example, spoke one language, held to one religion, followed one set of customs, but they had no central government. Each town was ruled by its own head chief, or *mico*, and was independent. However, the people who spoke a common language recognized a sort of kinship, usually did not fight each other, and often joined in a temporary confederacy against other tribes of different languages and customs.

Early settlers spoke of the head chiefs as "kings," and they were not too far wrong. The chiefs had strong authority and were greatly respected. Some, like the head of the Natchez, who was a true king, were carried on litters and wore special insignia. Their wives might be similarly honored. In most cases the chief's rule was not hereditary, however; a man attained high rank through demonstrating his superior fitness for it.

The head chiefs were not primarily warriors, although, of course, it was not likely that a man could become a chief unless he had proved himself in war. Among the overwhelming majority of Indian tribes in North America that were ruled by chiefs, those who governed were not war chiefs, but were selected for their wisdom and general ability. There were war chiefs as well, but their business was to lead the fighting, not to govern. In this the Indians had the same government structure as our own, with the military subordinate to the civilian.

The Southeasterners had a system of clans, with descent traced through the mother. A man belonged to his mother's clan. Usually he went to live with his wife's people when he married. Very often, men married women from other towns, and this helped

16th century Florida chief; elaborate tattooing shows his rank

A 16th century Florida warrior armed with a wicked war club

Cherokee Indian by Catlin, drawn after the tribe had been moved to Oklahoma

27

Billy Bowlegs, a minor Seminole war chief, on the warpath. The artist got Bowlegs' head and shoulders from a photograph, but the rest of the picture came from his imagination and has no connection with reality

to tie a tribe together. In theory, a man could marry several wives, but since he lived surrounded by his first wife's relatives, usually he could do so only if she agreed. Some of the Southeastern tribes, such as the Creeks, had a taboo that is found in many other parts of North America. This was the "mother-in-law taboo." It required that the husband and his mother-in-law never speak to each other, in many cases never even see each other. Instead, the two might send each other gifts from time to time.

There was a definite code of law, although a rather primitive one. When a murder occurred, the dead man's relatives were free to kill the murderer. Sometimes, if the murderer was a great chief, a less important man of his clan would be named to be killed in his place—provided the victim's people could catch him. One young warrior was thus named to be the scapegoat for a famous war chief. He solved his problem by killing the chief himself. Everyone agreed that this was perfectly fair, and, since the chief had been a great and strong warrior, that the young man had performed a brave act.

The Southeasterners had a noble religion, lived comfortably, made good pottery, wove remarkably fine cloth out of thread spun from wild fibers, cultivated large fields. Much in their lives was gracious and beautiful. But war was their "beloved occupa-

An 18th century sketch of Choctaw Indians. The two men are painted for the warpath and carry scalps on their staffs. The seated figure with the feather crown may be a Natchez chief

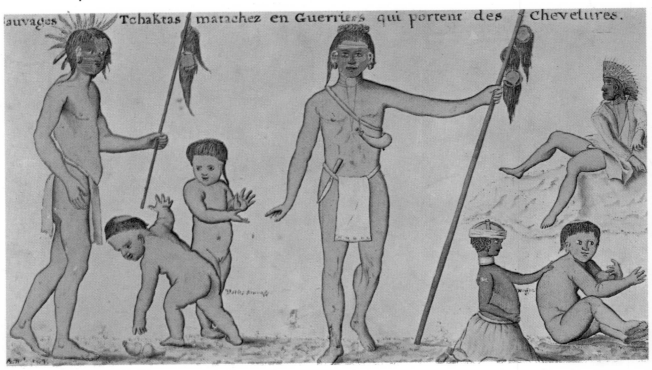

Model of a prehistoric council meeting in a ceremonial earth lodge, reconstructed from archaeologists' excavations. The heavy red and white body paint is based in part on observations of historic Indians. The orator carries a fan of white feathers

tion." It was spoken of as the greatest of delights, and it was practiced with the utmost cruelty. When the people were not at war they spoke of themselves as being idle. On one occasion, when the British urged the Cherokees to make peace with the Catawbas, the Cherokees protested that if they did, it would be necessary for them to start a war with another tribe, as otherwise they would be idle and would not know what to do with themselves.

They did not wage war as we understand the term. As a rule, they did not seek conquest, try to subjugate other tribes, or drive them out of their territories. What they wanted was to run risks and kill people for the sheer sport of it.

The typical mode of fighting was the raid. The war party, which was usually smaller than the fighting power of the town it planned to attack, prepared itself for the raid by dancing and praying. Then the warriors stole quietly through the woods and made a sudden, murderous attack just before dawn. A favorite trick was to set the roofs of the enemy's houses afire with burning arrows, then rush in and kill the townspeople as they ran out in disorder.

The preferred weapons were spears and clubs that could be used in close combat. Using these involved

considerable risk, and better displayed the warrior's courage. The Indians were, however, competent archers, using an efficient longbow that shot long arrows (the short bows usually shown as Indian came into use after the bowmen acquired horses and began shooting from horseback). But a bow is meant for killing from a distance and so its use involved less risk and consequently brought less honor.

Killing women and children was as highly regarded as killing men, since to get to them one had to enter the town. However, women and children were occasionally taken prisoner and adopted into the enemy tribe. Warrior prisoners were also sometimes spared

Creek chief Coosa Tustennuggee's pipe tomahawk, of a type that was widely traded by white men to Indians

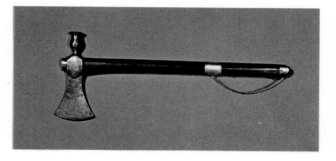

Choctaw Eagle Dance; this picture was painted by Catlin in the 1830's in Oklahoma

and adopted, but this was rare except among the Natchez, who kept up their strength by adopting boys and young men into the Stinker half of the tribe. With most of the Southeasterners, adult males were captured for only one purpose—to torture them. For this reason, young male prisoners in good condition were hard to come by; a reasonable man would sooner die fighting than let himself be taken.

When a town captured a prisoner, everyone was delighted. First the victorious warriors cleansed themselves from the magical influences of battle, after

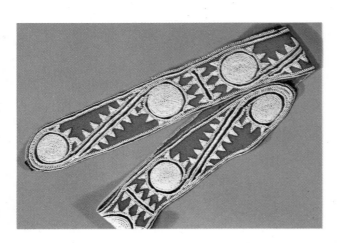

which the captive was tied to a pole in the town center and carefully and elaborately tortured to death. This procedure had about it the curious character of a competition. The victim sang his war songs, taunted his captors, did everything he could to infuriate them and show his superior courage. The torturers, who were mostly women, did their best to break him down before he died.

This torture complex, the deep relish on the part of men and women in inflicting the most extreme pain, is difficult to explain. A love of fighting for the excitement of it and as a road to glory is found among many peoples; in Europe, in the Middle Ages, it was elaborated into the rituals of chivalry. But delight in torture is rare in most civilizations. Yet in their other relationships the Southeasterners were not especially cruel or unkind. They were as fond of laughter as anybody, capable of kindness and of love.

They played many games, which they called "the little brother of war"; the games were usually rough.

Choctaw beaded wool belt, early 20th century. The circular "scroll" design is traditional with these people

30

The contestants prepared to play them with fasting and prayer. The most important game, which is still played by some surviving tribes such as the Choctaws, was the original of lacrosse. Lacrosse as we play it today, with teams of fixed sides, many rules, and umpires, is still no game for sissies. In its native, crude form it provided a splendid way to run risks and break heads, all in a spirit of fun.

It is a common observation in the course of history that warlike, aggressive tribes and nations are people of above-average energy and ability. A good example of this is the early Romans, who started out pretty much as land pirates and developed into not only conquerors, but engineers, lawmakers, and perhaps the greatest carriers of civilization that the world has ever known. It may be that at certain stages of development some tribes and nations have more energy than they can use up, and they find in warfare the outlet they need. Then when other outlets appear or are discovered, the same energy and ability go into them.

The Choctaw game of lacrosse is shown in the Catlin painting below. Above is a ball player, also by Catlin, carrying lacrosse sticks and in ceremonial costume

William McIntosh, head chief of the Lower Creeks. He was executed by his people on May 1, 1825, for ceding Creek lands to the U.S. without the people's approval

Certainly the great tribes of the Southeast responded vigorously to the effects of contact with European civilization. Many of the lesser tribes, such as the Natchez and the Timucuas, are extinct; the white men were too much for them. Others survive today as mixed-blood remnants, little more than a handful of families who have kept almost nothing of their old culture or tribal existence except a memory. The great tribes, however, came closer than has any other group of American Indians to making the adjustment that would have enabled them to survive on their native ground as the equals of the white men who surrounded them. These are the tribes that later became known as the "Five Civilized Tribes"—the Cherokees, Choctaws, Chickasaws, and Creeks, plus the Seminoles, a branch of the Creeks that broke away from the main tribe after the coming of the white men.

The English were settling on the Atlantic Coast. The Spanish had established themselves in Florida. The French, after various attempts in Florida and farther north, concentrated their settlements in the area around New Orleans and upward along the Mississippi. All three nations courted the great tribes. Had the four tribes, as they then numbered, been able to forget their ancient enmities and unite against the white men, they could have controlled absolutely the history of the Southeast. As it was, their friendships or enmities swayed the balance of power among the European nations.

The English established an alliance with the Creeks, and relatively good relations with the Cherokees and Chickasaws. The French allied themselves with the Choctaws—and the Natchez, while they lasted. The tribe nearest the Spanish was the Seminole, but while there was much trade and interchange between the two groups, the Seminoles gave the Spanish no positive alliance, and so put them at a disadvantage.

The Indian chiefs visited the Europeans' settlements, dealt with their governors and councils. Some of them, especially the allies of the English, were taken overseas to meet the white men's kings. They saw their clothing and possessions, their houses, their cattle, their crafts, their organization, and their use of slaves, and began to copy them. The Indian cos-

Coosa Tustennuggee, a Creek chief; one of a series of 19th century Indian portraits painted in Washington

*James Oglethorpe, the founder of Georgia, presenting the Creek chief Tomochichi and
other Indians to the Lord Trustees of the Colony of Georgia in 1734 in London*

tume changed radically. Many Indians began building more solid houses. They acquired cattle. They
learned the use of the spinning wheel. They obtained
firearms and ploughs. They bought slaves. The
Creeks began to tighten their organization into a
confederacy intended to unite all the towns of the
tribe. The great tribes became stronger and more
prosperous than ever before in their history.

Then the English conquered Canada, and most of
the French empire in the New World collapsed. The
Spanish were weak, and soon to quit Florida. The
five tribes found that they had no choice but to deal
with England. As in their relations with the Iroquois
farther north, the English saw in these Indians an
important factor in maintaining their empire against
hostile tribes to the west, the threat of the Spanish in
the Southwest, and the possibility of a renewal of

French ambitions. Under English influence, the
Creeks further tightened their confederacy and dominated the Cherokees and Choctaws.

Then the colonies revolted against the Crown. The
Creeks, loyal to their alliance, fought for England
and were defeated. As the tide of war favored the
colonists, the English abruptly pulled out of all the
territory south of Canada. The great tribes were
stranded; the alliance was dead.

Suddenly the Indians were confronted by a new
nation of hardy people who were interested only in
the land the tribes occupied. The Americans pressed
westward. All along the line west of the white men's
frontier, from the Great Lakes to the Gulf, the Indians began to realize that they were in danger, and
that no words, spoken or written, would stop this
new, unbelievably powerful tribe.

33

Osceola, the famous chief of the Seminoles, who led them in their final war against the whites and put up one of the stiffest resistances Indians ever made. This portrait was painted by George Catlin in the 1830's

The great Shawnee chief, Tecumseh, sought to unite the western and southeastern tribes in a war against the settlers. He visited the five tribes and tried to persuade them to join him. The Cherokees and Choctaws refused to make war; the Chickasaws held back. The Creeks were divided, and did not join him. Nevertheless, many of the Creek towns started war against the white men on their own until, in 1814, Andrew Jackson crushed them.

A short time later the Seminoles went on the war-path, and Jackson marched against them. The Seminoles were led by the famous chief Osceola, and under him put up a terrific resistance. Eventually their main strength was broken, but bands that refused to give up freedom held out in the swamps and forests of Florida. For a time the U. S. Army and Navy joined in a plan to exterminate the free Seminoles. They used thousands of men, spent millions of dollars, murdered a lot of Indians—and finally had to give up. To this day in Florida there are bands of Seminoles who claim, truthfully, that they have never surrendered to the United States.

The five tribes realized that they could never stand off the white men by force. The only hope was to learn their arts and become accepted by them as civilized people. The Cherokees and Creeks especially made great efforts to prove themselves to be peaceful, industrious, and progressive, worthy of the full protection of our laws.

The tribes invited missionaries to settle among them and open schools. The missionaries, convinced that the Indian tongue could not be written, taught only in English, using outdated methods. The teaching went slowly and the Indians were disappointed to find that after a year of study their children could read only a little English.

Among the Cherokees was an extraordinary man named Sequoyah. He did not attend the schools, but he hung around them and studied the primers. Then he set to work to invent a system of writing. The Cherokees suspected him of witchcraft; they burned his cabin, and all his papers with it. Disillusioned, he left the Cherokee country with a group who were seeking a place where they could get away from white men entirely, crossed the Mississippi, and settled in Arkansas.

Seminole hat, made in the early 1900's by Billy Bowlegs, a descendant of a minor but well-known Seminole chief. It is a reconstruction of the old style of hat

Seminole women and child of the present day. Left, a modern Choctaw drummer photographed in Oklahoma

Costume of a Seminole in 1857. Although sketched in Oklahoma, the costume was the same in Florida

The campaign to exterminate the Seminoles. This naive contemporary picture is a work of pure imagination, but does give some idea of the ferocity with which the Seminole War was conducted. Bloodhounds were used for tracking Indians, but it is doubtful that any performed as shown here

Typical chiki or summer sleeping house of the Seminoles

In 1821 Sequoyah returned to the main tribe, bringing with him a *written message* from the Arkansas group. He had invented a form of alphabet, using partly Roman characters (without regard to the values we give them), and partly new characters that he had made up. For all the fact that the system was clumsy, it was neatly adapted to writing the Cherokee language.

Sequoyah, the inventor of the Cherokee alphabet. He is wearing a medal awarded him for his achievement

Cherokee Alphabet.

Dₐ	Rₑ	Tᵢ	Ꮆₒ	Oᵤ	iᵥ
Ꮜgₐ Ꮎkₐ	Ᏺgₑ	Ᏻgᵢ	Aₘ	Jgᵤ	Egᵥ
Ꮚhₐ	Ꮅhₑ	Ꭿhᵢ	Ᏺhₒ	Ꭺhᵤ	Ꮣhᵥ
Wₗₐ	Ꮄₗₑ	Ꮈₗᵢ	Gₗₒ	Mₗᵤ	Ꭵₗᵥ
Ꮆₘₐ	Ꭴₘₑ	Hₘᵢ	ꝝₘₒ	Yₘᵤ	
Ꮎₙₐ ᏆₜₕₙₐGₙₐₕ	Ʌₙₑ	ｈₙᵢ	Zₙₒ	ꝗₙᵤ	Oₙᵥ
Ꮖqᵤₐ	Ꮙqᵤₑ	Ꝑqᵤᵢ	Ꮿqᵤₒ	ꞷqᵤᵤ	Ᏼqᵤᵥ
Ꮜₛₐ ꝋₛ	4ₛₑ	ｂₛᵢ	ꝉₛₒ	Ꝑₛᵤ	Rₛᵥ
Ꮮdₐ Wₜₐ	Ꮝdₑ Ꮤₜₑ	ᏗdᵢᏋₜᵢ	Ʌdₒ	Sdᵤ	Ꮷdᵥ
Ꭷdₗₐꮎₜₗₐ	Lₜₗₑ	Cₜₗᵢ	ꝝₜₗₒ	Ꝟₜₗᵤ	Pₜₗᵥ
Gₜₛₐ	Vₜₛₑ	Ꭱₜₛᵢ	Kₜₛₒ	Jₜₛᵤ	Cꭳₜₛᵥ
Gwₐ	ꞷwₑ	Ꝋwᵢ	Ꝍwₒ	Ꝥwᵤ	6wᵥ
ꞷyₐ	Ᏸyₑ	Ꭿyᵢ	ｈyₒ	Gꭳyᵤ	Byᵥ

Sounds represented by Vowels

a, as *a* in *father*, or short as a in *rival*   o, as *aw* in *law*, or short as o in *not*.
e, as *a* in *hate*, or short as *e* in *met*   u, as *oo* in *fool*, or short as u in *pull*.
i, as *i* in *pique*, or short as i in *pit*   v, as *u* in *but*, nasalized.

Consonant Sounds

g nearly as in English, but approaching to k. d nearly as in English but approaching to t. h k l m n q s t w y, as in English. Syllables beginning with g, except Ꮝ have sometimes the power of k, Ꮜ, Ꮝ, Ꮗ, are sometimes sounded to, tu, tv, and Syllables written with tl except Ꮣ sometimes vary to dl.

At first the Cherokees paid no attention to him, but finally, after further demonstrations, they were convinced. What happened then was astounding. Everyone wanted to read and write. Old men, young warriors, housewives, old women at the spinning wheels, farmers when they rested from ploughing, boys and girls studied the alphabet. Young men went on trips just to show off by writing a girl a letter. In a matter of months, virtually every Cherokee not an infant or feebleminded could read and write.

The Creeks took up the writing. The Bible was printed in the Cherokee and Creek languages; the Cherokees published a newspaper. Most of the five tribes put their laws in writing; the Cherokees wrote a formal constitution.

At times the Five Civilized Tribes, as they were now becoming, invited white men to help them, but the great progress they made was their own. They developed their industries; they became peaceful. They farmed in the white men's manner and kept cattle. In the southern, fertile areas, many of their farms were real plantations, complete with slaves. With the Cherokees in the lead, the Indians were doing something that has seldom happened in all history: they were proving that a relatively primitive people can, on their own initiative, catch up with a greatly more advanced civilization in short order.

As the Indians turned to more extensive farming and, with livestock, became less dependent on hunting, larger populations were able to live decently on smaller areas of land. Had enough white Americans of those days believed that Indians were entitled to the same justice that they themselves cherished, an Indian state might have come peacefully into the Union in a few generations. But the white men could not let this happen. They wanted the Indians' land; they envied the prosperous farms and plantations.

Then gold was discovered inside some of the tribal territories. That settled it. Between 1832 and 1839, by bribery, by persuasion, by fraud, and above all, by brutal force, the Indians of the Five Civilized Tribes were driven out of their homelands and moved to Oklahoma—a far, strange, unfriendly land. Several chiefs who had been bribed into signing away the tribal lands were killed by their own people. Thousands of Indians, men, women, and children, died on the "Trail of Tears" leading away from their homeland. Not a few were shot or bayoneted trying to defend their homes, or as an example to others who were slow to move out.

Not all the Indians went. A fair number of Cherokees hid out in the mountains of North Carolina, and now occupy the Qualla reservation in that state, on land largely purchased with their own money. Some of the Choctaws eluded the troops, and remain scattered on small tracts of land in Mississippi. Nobody even tried to move the unconquered Seminole bands in the Florida wilderness; they had stung us too often.

In a strange, new land, harassed from time to time by wild tribes and by white outlaws, the Five Civilized Tribes set to work. They tamed the land, planted their farms, built up herds of livestock. They set up competent, modern governments. Once again they got the printing press going. They established a public school system. They were back on their feet.

But when the Civil War started, the Five Civilized Tribes, who were southerners, sided with the South. That gave the government an excuse to tear up the old treaties and make new, harsher ones. Even this was not enough. The white men were moving ever farther west, and some of Oklahoma was fine country. Eventually the Indian territory was broken up, the self-government system of the Five Civilized Tribes was destroyed, and an end was put to the last traces of an experiment in the ability of a group of American Indians to civilize themselves.

The Cherokee chief Stalking Turkey, painted while he was on a trip to London in 1762 by Francis Parsons

Cherokee coat. The manner in which it is cut comes, of course, from European models

Dance mask of the Cherokees

Decorated Cherokee bag. The bag and the coat at left were both probably made before 1835

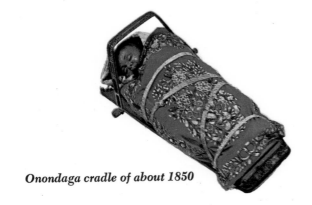

Onondaga cradle of about 1850

The Iroquoians

Iroquois False Face Society mask. When colored red, a mask is considered particularly powerful. This mask, although it is not an old one, is in the traditional style

The spread of the beginnings of civilization northward from the Gulf Coast can be pictured as being like a tree, its roots in the south, its top in the north, its branches spreading east and west, top and branches becoming slimmer, the foliage less thick, toward the tips. The top of the tree, just reaching into Canada, was made up of a group of tribes speaking a language related to Cherokee. When the first European explorers came among these people, their culture was distinctly less advanced than that of the Southeasterners, but still well ahead of the tribes around them, whose territory they had invaded.

These invaders spoke dialects of the language we call Iroquois. In this book we shall speak of the Iroquois-speaking tribes as a whole as "Iroquoians," although that term really includes the Cherokees, and keep the term "Iroquois" for the particular group of tribes that became united in the League of the Iroquois, which will be described later.

When the French first came to the New World, they found the Iroquoians in Ohio, Pennsylvania, New York, and in some of the country across the St. Lawrence River in Canada. They centered upon the eastern Great Lakes and the St. Lawrence, in territory from which they had driven the earlier, Algonkian-speaking tribes. The Algonkians lived in the terri-

Huron buckskin moccasins with dyed moose hair embroidery showing French influence

Onondaga basket with design stamped with carved potato

A 20th century woven basketry turkey, Seneca

Eagle Dance of the Senecas painted by Ernest Smith, a contemporary Seneca artist. The dress shows the influence of the white men, being largely of woven material; the men wear their hair long instead of shaved close — a fairly recent practice

tory surrounding that of the Iroquois, and feared and hated them; the name "Iroquois" comes from an Algonkian word meaning "real adders."

The Iroquoians had taken over a rich and fertile land. They farmed on a large scale, raising squashes, fifteen varieties of corn, and no less than sixty kinds of beans. Wild strawberries, wild greens and herbs, and maple sugar were also part of their diet. The men cleared the fields for planting, cutting down and burning the trees; thereafter the farming was done by the women. This was not quite so unfair an arrangement as it might seem, since the fields and crops belonged to the women.

The women did much of their farming in groups, helping each other and making a social occasion of the work. So, too, the men liked to hunt in parties. They hunted deer, trapped beaver, killed duck, turkey, and wild pigeons, and fished in dammed streams, working with very large nets made of vines.

The Iroquoians lived in compact villages surrounded by strong, wooden stockades. The houses, which were built by the men but belonged to the women, were of two types—buildings with rounded roofs, rather like Quonset huts, and structures called "longhouses" with pitched roofs. Both buildings were covered with elm bark, laid on like clapboards. A longhouse was up to 100 feet long and sheltered many families of one clan. Extending down the center of the building was a row of fires, with a smoke hole over each. To the right and left of each fire was a room which was the home of one family. By all accounts the longhouses were smoky and noisy, and the dogs that lived with the families must have been a nuisance. Yet the houses were warm and waterproof.

Elm bark, which was used for the walls and roofs, was important in many ways to the Iroquoians. Theirs was not good birchbark country, so they used elm for their utensils, and even made canoes out of

Painting showing the village life and activities of the Iroquoians of prehistoric and early historic times. Villages of this type were often surrounded by a stout stockade of wooden stakes to give them protection in case of sudden enemy attack

Onondaga pot from about A.D. *1450*

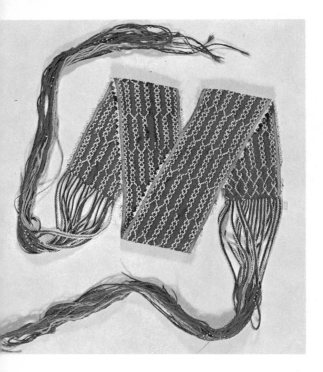

Iroquois woven woolen sash, probably Seneca

Basket made by the Onondagas

it. Elm-bark canoes were heavy and clumsy and could not be carried from one lake or river to another. However, they had one advantage in warfare. When the Iroquoians attacked the stockaded village of an enemy tribe, the canoes could be upended against the stockade and the warriors could climb up the rough bark and enter the village.

The Iroquoians' arts were not nearly so fine as those of the Southeast, but they were interesting nonetheless. They included a smooth, decorated pottery, better than the Algonkians', and attractive sashes made by a form of weaving that continues to this day. (Nowadays the work is done with cotton and wool; the original materials were probably wild fibers.) The Iroquoians also developed the use of the delicate shell beads called wampum to a high pitch, though it is not likely they made their own since they lived so far from the coast where clamshells, from which the beads were made, are found. Instead, they probably got them in trade, by raiding, or as tribute.

Strings of wampum were carried by Iroquoian messengers as a form of identification. Belts or strips of it, in various designs, could serve as simple documents. Strings of various lengths and with different arrangements of light and dark beads served as reminders of legends, history, and treaties. Specialists were trained to memorize the meanings of a number of strings and belts, so that as they handled them they recalled the matters recorded by the wampum. These men were in a sense living libraries, able to

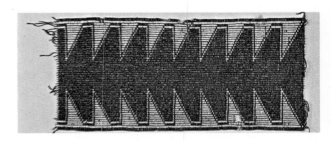

Above, the Dust Fan wampum belt, symbol of the presiding officer of the Iroquois League; below, the belt that records the adoption of the Tuscaroras into the League

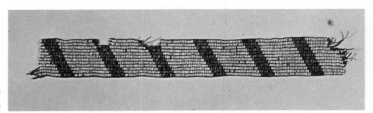

recite great quantities of important history as they ran their fingers over the beads.

The Iroquoians lived in a land of hard, snowy winters. The men when fully dressed wore leggings, breechclouts, and kilts of buckskin, moccasins, and buckskin shirts. In summer this dress might be reduced to breechclout, kilt, and moccasins. The women wore skirts and leggings in warm weather, and full-length dresses when it was cooler.

The combination of leggings and breechclout, plus a kilt to cover the gap between the two, is found over a large part of North America. It is as close as most Indians came to trousers, which require much more difficult cutting, fitting, and sewing. Sewing through even the softest hides with bone awls or thorns is hard work, as is cutting with stone knives, so it is not surprising they were satisfied with the easier combination. Trousers and fitted shirts originated in the Arctic; the Eskimos wore them, as did all the Arctic people clear to the coast of Europe. Such nations as the Romans were in touch with people who had been wearing trousers for hundreds of years, but they preferred to wrap themselves in fancy robes which they called togas. It was not until the betrousered northerners overran them that the Romans adopted fitted clothing.

The Indians went part way, making the relatively simple leggings. Many tribes, however, learned to fashion well-fitting shirts and women's dresses of buckskin, often slashing the excess buckskin to form a decorative fringe.

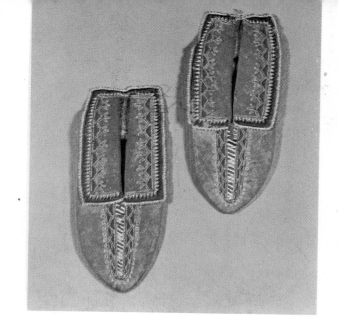

Moccasins in the traditional style, with beadwork decoration, made by the Senecas

Seneca earrings, examples of Iroquois silverwork. Until the white men arrived, the Iroquois knew nothing of metals. Thereafter they became skilled in working them

The Totadaho belt (below) graphically records the bristling resistance of the Onondaga chief Totadaho to his tribe's joining the Iroquois League. The overcoming of his objections permitted the League to come into being

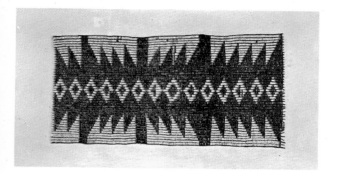

Seneca leggings. Leggings similar to these were made by other Iroquoians and by coastal Algonkian tribes

*Masks used by the Iroquoians in their ceremonies and festivals. Some, such as the wooden
False Faces, had strong religious significance. Others were used when dancing for fun*

The Iroquoians took religion seriously, worked hard at it, and wove it into every moment of their lives. Spirits of all sorts abounded, affecting everything they did. In addition to the spirits and the ever-present ghosts of the dead, there were divine beings whom we can well call gods: above all the Master of Life, from whom came all good things, and his opposite and brother who was the maker of evil. The good god and his evil brother were in constant struggle.

A human being consisted of three parts: his body; what we may call his soul; and his spirit or ghost. When he died, his soul departed for the afterlife which was a kind of heaven. The ghost, as distinct from the spirit, remained near the place of burial and continued to share in the life of the living. War parties, for example, might be accompanied by great flocks of dead warriors who wished to share in the excitement. Feasts were given in the wintertime, at which the barriers between living and dead were broken down and the ghosts shared in the food, the dancing, the games, and the warmth.

There was another form of spirit, the idea of which is difficult for white men to understand, since most of us find it hard to grasp the thought of a spiritual power that is completely impersonal. This the Iroquoians called "orenda." It pervaded all things, and

was the sacred or divine essence that related all the elements of the world to each other—men included. A concept of this sort is common to many North American Indian tribes.

Orenda was achieved chiefly through significant dreams which gave a man strength for his daily life as well as for sacred matters. Certain men could accumulate more orenda than others. Those who dreamed powerfully enough became shamans with power to cure sickness. Equally important were the men who dealt with the False Faces, which were horrible heads without bodies that appeared to people in the forests and bewitched them into sickness. The members of the False Face Society broke the evil spell by a ceremony in which they themselves wore wooden masks carved in the likeness of the False Faces.

Shamans with magical powers are often found among hunting tribes. Among agricultural tribes, major ceremonies were usually conducted by carefully trained men who are more properly called priests. The Iroquoians had both.

Their most important ceremony was the great New Year Festival in the month Diagona, the second moon after the winter solstice—that is, in late January or early February. This was the dead of winter, when the time was approaching for the Master of Life to

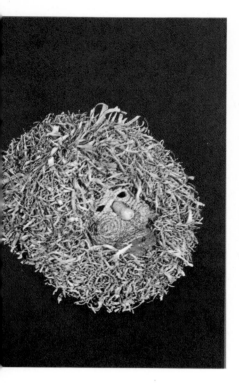
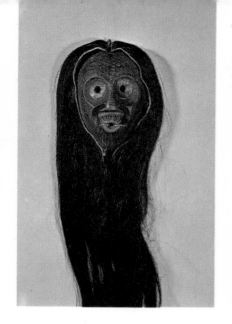

In addition to the masks they carved from wood, the Iroquoians also braided masks from corn husks. Such masks were important for their symbolism, not for their beauty

bring back the spring or for his evil brother to prevent its arrival. The rituals to help the Master went on for days. At the beginning, old fires were scattered and new ones laid, similar to the "new fire" ceremony of the Southeast. There were many rituals of cleansing, many prayers, and a re-enactment of the gambling contest in which, when the world was young, the Master of Life won spring and green growth and all good things from the forces of evil.

In the course of the ceremony, dreams were related. Some men, if they wished, narrated their dreams in public. However, since the Iroquoians believed that dreams betrayed one's secret wishes and guilty acts, most preferred to tell them under strictest secrecy to trained men who interpreted them, practicing a primitive but real form of psychoanalysis. They also believed that certain dreams must be obeyed, and it was considered dangerous to let a lot of dreams pile up inside a person.

At this ceremony the matrons, the heads of the longhouses, gave new names to adults who had earned them. There was solemn ritual dancing, there was dancing for fun. There were games, clowning, even a form of charades.

It is interesting to note that this festival was held in the worst of winter. The crops had long been harvested. The men had done their fall hunting and

fishing, and after the snow lay deep and the bitter cold was all around, they kept pretty much to the crowded houses. Everyone was cooped up; day in and day out, everyone saw too much of everyone else. Supplies of fresh food were gone. Shortly the winter would break, the sap begin to rise in the sugar maples. For this feast the men had to bestir themselves and hunt, and disagreeable though it might have been it did them good. Then everyone cut loose in a mixture of fun and solemn piety. The result must have been a great relaxing of tensions.

Like a number of other primitive peoples, the Iroquoians gave women a higher position than they enjoyed among white men until recent times. The fields, the crops, the houses belonged to them. This meant that they had the upper hand economically. Descent was traced through the woman; a child belonged to its mother's clan. The people all belonged to clans, such as Wolf, Deer, Turtle, and Snipe. The animal "totem" of the clan was shown over the door of each longhouse, which was occupied by members of one clan plus their husbands. Men went to live with their wives when they married. If the marriage broke up, it was the man who went home to mother, leaving his children behind him.

The clans of the Seneca, Cayuga, and Onondaga tribes were also grouped into moieties, or halves.

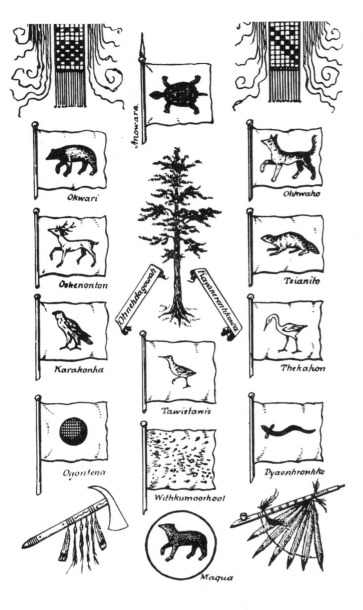

Snowara.

Okwari

Oskenonton

Karakonha

Ogontena

Ohnehdagowah Kayaneronhkowa

Tawistawis

Withkumoorhool

Maqua

Ohkwaho

Tsianito

Thekahon

Dyaonhronhko

One moiety consisted of the Turtle clan plus all clans named after four-footed animals except Deer. The other was made up of the Deer clan and all clans named after birds. Members of one moiety always married members of the other, and the moieties performed various services for each other, especially burying the other's dead. The two moieties competed in various games, among them a form of lacrosse much like that played by the Southeastern tribes.

Each clan was divided into "lineages" of members descended from a common ancestor. At the head of each lineage was an older woman, the matron. Certain lineages were—and still are—"noble"; from them the chiefs, or sachems, were chosen. "Sachem" is an Algonkian word, but is commonly used for the ruling Iroquoian chiefs.

When a sachem died, the matron of his lineage chose a successor from that lineage. She then talked her choice over with the other women of her longhouse, then of her clan. Undoubtedly the choice had been thoroughly discussed before it was publicly announced, because when it was, the women of her clan almost always ratified it. The matron then got the approval of her moiety, then of the opposite one, which was probably little more than a formality. When the period of mourning for the dead chief drew to a close, an elaborate ceremony was held to formally end the mourning and to install the new sachem, who received the deer's horns which were the mark of his office. In accordance with the rules, he gave up warfare entirely. The new official received the old one's name and his orenda and became in some degree a continuation of the man himself and all those who had held the office before him.

Rum casks, as on these two Wyandot pipes of 1800-1825, became common in Indian art

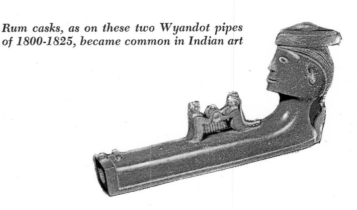

If a sachem failed in his duties, the matron warned him three times. If he still did not improve, she would "remove the horns" by asking the council to depose him, which the council seldom failed to do. The matrons also could propose matters for the council to consider. The women did not rule, they did not give orders, but they had a good deal of influence over the men who did.

The Iroquoian customs with respect to captives showed Southeastern influence and involved revolting cruelty. In combat, they took as many prisoners as they could. Young men were preferred, but women and children were also captured. On the way back to the captors' village these unfortunates were driven as we would not drive cattle and killed if they lagged. When the survivors reached the village, the inhabitants armed themselves with sticks and clubs and formed two lines, between which the prisoners had to run while the people beat and clubbed them for all they were worth. Then the council parceled them out among the women of families that had recently lost members.

Usually, women and old men were kept pretty much as slaves. Children were likely to be adopted. The matrons decided whether warriors should be kept to replace men who had died, or be tortured to death. If they were kept, they became loyal members of their new tribe. Strangely, a man's native tribe thought none the worse of him for having thus joined the enemy.

Torturing prisoners slowly to death seems to have been more definitely regarded as a religious sacrifice by the Iroquoians than by the Southeastern tribes. The concept of a sacrifice, in fact, suggests that here in the far North an item of influence from Mexico had been kept in fairly pure form. The offering was made to Areskoi, spirit of war and hunting and perhaps also of the sun. When no male captive was available, a woman prisoner might be sacrificed, as is indicated in the wording of a sacrificial prayer recorded long ago, in which Areskoi was told, ". . . we offer thee this victim whom we burn for thee, that thou mayest be filled with her flesh, and render us ever anew victorious over our enemies."

The victim was regarded with respect, even with affection. On one occasion observed by white men, a group of young men and women who had slipped off into the woods during the torture of an enemy warrior were rebuked by a sachem for showing lack of respect toward the man who was so bravely entertaining the people. Like the Southeasterners, Iroquoian captives did their level best to prove that they were too much men for their captors to break down. They acted as if their fate was a high honor. They feasted with their captors, danced and sang for them, conversed with them between agonies, and ridiculed and defied them while the torments were being applied.

In the war between the League of the Iroquois and the Hurons, which finally ended in the destruction of the latter, an Iroquois prisoner named Saouandanancous was brought in by the Hurons. His hands were seriously injured. He was turned over to a lineage in which a young man, son of an old chief, had recently been killed. After the captive had been feasted, the chief addressed him with true sorrow. He had hoped the Iroquois could replace his son, but when he saw how his hands had been ruined, he knew this could not be. "So take courage," said the Huron, "and prepare to die tonight like a brave man."

The prisoner was fed and tenderly cared for all through the day. From the original account, it is clear that many of the Hurons felt compassion for him and wished there were some way to change his fate. However, it could not be. He was killed by fire in such a manner that it took over twelve hours; throughout, as each Huron applied the particular pain he had decided upon, the prisoner was addressed courteously and lovingly. During one of the intervals when he was revived and allowed to rest he gave his

torturers news of the Hurons who had been adopted into the Iroquois tribe; during another he sang. When death finally came his body was carved up and distributed among the tribe. The Iroquoians frequently ended their sacrifice with cannibalism—not out of a fondness for human flesh, but to absorb some of the bravery of a courageous victim.

It is a curious riddle how so dreadful a custom could be practiced by the Iroquoians. Undoubtedly the sacrifice, the feasting of the victim, and the cannibalism came up from the South and originally from Mexico. Yet unlike the tribes of the South, who killed for sport or enjoyment, the Iroquoians inflicted their unspeakable cruelty on victims whom they pitied and admired.

The Iroquoians may have taken this custom for granted; it did not sit so well on white men or on the Algonkian tribes. Some Algonkians in revenge learned torture from the Iroquoians, thus spreading the custom. Mostly it was the Iroquoians they tortured, when they could capture them (the victim must have regarded this as a social comedown). However, the Iroquoians were the worst offenders in the North. The practice made them hated and feared, and gave them an evil name that has since been applied to Indians in general.

Five hundred years ago, the Iroquoian tribes were in constant warfare with each other. They seem to have had the Southeastern tradition of leagues or confederacies, and from time to time two or more

tribes worked out alliances, but they could not establish a broad peace among themselves. Part of their trouble was a deadly system of blood feuds; if a man was killed, even accidentally, a man of the tribe that had killed him must die, whereupon that tribe, in turn, had to kill a man of the first tribe, and so on and on. Only a few incidents were needed to involve the Iroquoians in a hopeless sequence of killing and of ever greater hatred. The situation was serious, especially for those tribes, such as the Mohawks, which had powerful Algonkian enemies as neighbors. Often, when Iroquoian warriors were off attacking their brethren, the Algonkians would swoop down on the home village and create havoc.

Not long before the white men came to North America, five nations of the Iroquois organized their famous League, which they called "The Great Peace." The idea started with a prophet called Deganawida, who had a vision of a great spruce tree with its top reaching through the sky to the land of the Master of Life. The tree stood for the sisterhood of all tribes, and its roots were the five Iroquois nations. An eagle perched at the top, keeping watch against any enemy that might come to break the peace.

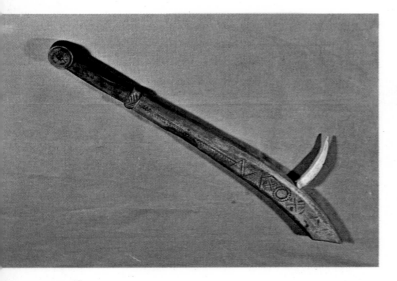

Spike war club dating from before 1850. The tribe is unknown, but this style of club was a widespread one

An engraving from a 1709 portrait of Brant, a Mohawk, grandfather of the Revolutionary leader Joseph Brant

Deganawida visualized the Great Peace as a sort of world federation. The teaching was religious and idealistic. Its members were to practice three pairs of principles—health of body and mind, and peace between individuals and tribes; right conduct and thought, and justice and respect for human rights; preparedness for defense, and keeping and increasing the spiritual power, orenda.

Deganawida's first follower was a practical-minded man, Hiawatha, to whom tradition gives principal credit for creating a working league. The real Hiawatha should not be confused with the hero of Longfellow's unfortunate poem, who resembles no real Indian, living or dead. The real Hiawatha, the statesman, united the Onondagas, Senecas, Cayugas, Oneidas, and Mohawks in a true union, the League of the Iroquois. In the eighteenth century they were joined by the Tuscaroras, Iroquoians who moved up from near the Cherokee country to escape the attacks of the white men. The League has lasted some four hundred years and is still functioning.

Blood feuds within the League were ended by establishing a system of payments to atone for a killing. If a quarrel arose between two member nations which they were unable to settle for themselves, it eventually came before the council of the League. Hiawatha's unwritten constitution knit together independent tribes so that they would face the rest of the world standing together, yet did not interfere with the management of strictly internal affairs. When the founding fathers wrote the U.S. Constitution, they had a similar problem to solve in uniting sovereign states. It is often claimed that they drew ideas from the League of the Iroquois; certainly a number of the framers of the Constitution were well acquainted with the League.

The council of the League was drawn from the sachems of the member tribes. It met each summer in the Onondaga country. When a matter had been thoroughly debated, the sachems of each tribe discussed it among themselves, for each group voted as a unit. A highly ceremonious system of discussing, voting, and, if need be, further discussion was followed, which was well designed to insure careful consideration and the greatest possible agreement.

Red Jacket, painted in New York in 1828. He wears a medal that was presented to him by George Washington

It was typical of Iroquois daring and high-mindedness to conceive of their confederacy as something that should embrace all the world they knew. The catch to this was that they thought of the Great Peace as an *Iroquois* peace in which the members of the League should be at the top. The only tribe received into the League as an equal was the Tuscarora, and it had to undergo some years of probation in an inferior position. The people of certain other tribes were told that they should become women and children, the men to give up being warriors entirely, the tribe to become totally dependent upon the League. Naturally, most tribes refused such a peace. About the only ones to accept it voluntarily were the Delawares, who had been driven from their homeland on the coast and desperately needed protection from the white men.

Mostly—and ironically—the Great Peace was spread by war. Iroquois imperialism was complicated by the struggle between member tribes and those outside the confederacy to control the very profitable fur trade, first with the French and Dutch, then the French and English, and by the even greater struggle between France and England for control of North America. In this second struggle, the English had the good fortune to become allied with the Iroquois in the north, as they were with the powerful Creeks in the south.

The Iroquois did not make such a cult of war as did the Southeasterners. Under the rule of the League, their warriors could raid only those tribes against whom the council had declared war. Nonetheless, they seldom stopped fighting. War was a young man's road to glory. Small parties went raiding, and sometimes a man set out alone to win fame. One such warrior, somewhat in the spirit of a stamp collector paying a high price for a rare specimen, traveled alone to Wisconsin, passing for days through enemy territory, to bring back a scalp from a tribe hitherto unknown.

As warfare grew more and more intense, fanned by the conflict over the fur trade and the imperial ambitions of France and Britain, the united Iroquois were able to put armies of five hundred or a thousand

Although made before the Revolution, this map was used to show the routes taken by the American generals Clinton and Sullivan in their raid on the Iroquois in 1779

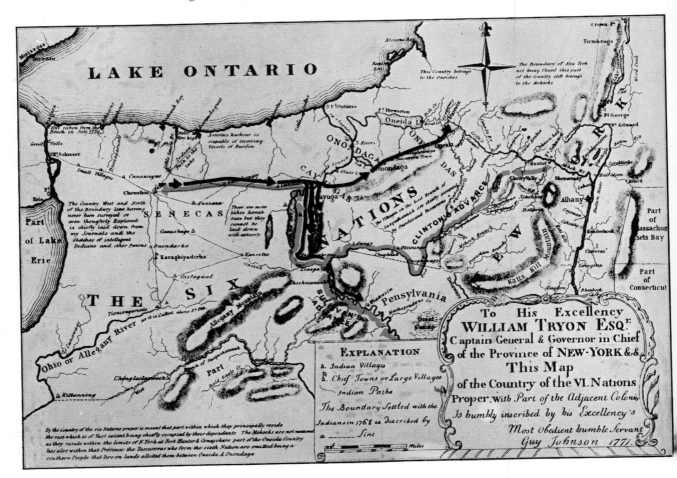

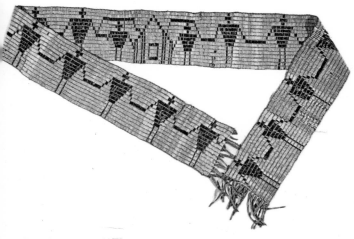

Washington wampum belt; it records the treaty between the Iroquois and Washington following the Revolution

men in the field, a scale of operations until then unknown in that part of the world. The French supported various Algonkian tribes and such Iroquoians as the Hurons, who were hostile to the League. One by one the Iroquois broke these tribes. In many instances, especially when dealing with Iroquoians, they adopted the survivors. In other cases the remnants of tribes remained on their own territory under Iroquois rule. At its height, shortly before the American Revolution, the Iroquois empire reached south to the edge of Tennessee and west to Illinois. Tribes even farther away paid tribute to the League.

The League tipped the balance in favor of the British in the French and Indian War. In the American Revolution the League did not declare war formally, but most of the nations were loyal to their alliance with Britain, raised Ned all over northern New York and the adjacent parts of Pennsylvania, and tied down hundreds of American fighting men. So long as the colonials were under British jurisdiction, they and the Iroquois were friends. With the Revolution, the colonials ceased being British and became Americans; for the first time, and for a brief period, they tasted the military power and the horror they had once turned loose against the French and against other Indian tribes.

After the Revolution, the British offered the Iroquois a reservation in Canada, to which many of them moved. As many, and perhaps more, preferred to stay in their home country. Some of the important wampum records went north with those who migrated, while other records were kept at home.

Joseph Brant, or Thayendanega, a Mohawk, the most famous Iroquois chief at the time of the Revolution. Following the Revolution, he was granted land in Canada

As a result, there is a contention today between the New York and Canadian Iroquois as to which group has the right to call a League council.

To the annoyance of many New Yorkers, who would have liked to see the Iroquois exterminated, George Washington made a just peace with the League. Washington's policy paid off importantly. During the War of 1812 the Shawnee chief, Tecumseh, with British backing, built up a formidable alliance of the tribes between Ohio and the Mississippi River that posed a real threat to the northern United States. This the Iroquois refused to join; their old alliance with Britain had ended, and their word was pledged to the new nation. Had the Iroquois thrown in with Tecumseh, the British troops and Indians combined might well have overrun the northern part of the country and brought the war to a very different ending.

During the nineteenth century, the Iroquois were talked into ceding a good deal of their land in the Northeast, and some of them were moved to Oklahoma and Wisconsin. About ten thousand of them, however, remain in New York State, still keeping their identity and still holding to the tradition of the Iroquois League.

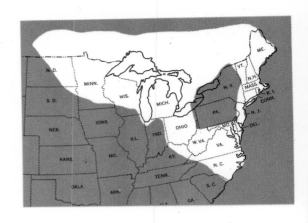

Chippewa beaded vest

The Wigwam People

Micmac birchbark boxes decorated with porcupine quills and (below) a Potawatomi bag with thunderbird design

Long before Iroquoian invaders began pushing up from the south, the northern part of the United States from the Atlantic to the Rocky Mountains must have been occupied by hunting tribes most of whom spoke languages of the Algonkian family. Algonkians also occupied all of eastern Canada except for the territory along the shores held by the Eskimos. There is good evidence that some of the ancestors of the Algonkians were very early settlers of the New World, people who reached the northeastern part of North America as long as 10,000 years ago.

Northwards of the country later conquered by the Iroquoians, in an arc from the Abenakis of Maine across to the Chippewas of western Ontario, Minnesota, and Wisconsin, were people living entirely or chiefly by hunting and fishing, whose way of life, even in recent times, gives a fair idea of how all the Algonkians once lived.

The tribes usually were broken up into widely scattered family groups or small bands, for better hunting; a whole tribe would get together only occasionally. Within the tribes and smaller groups, organization was loose and informal. Chiefs had little authority other than the respect given to their wisdom and experience. Despite their informal organization and general lack of authority, the hunters had a highly developed sense of land ownership. Not only did each tribe claim certain territory, but often each family claimed exclusive rights to hunt in an area of its own within that territory, which it guarded jealously against trespassers.

Late 16th century engraving showing how fish were speared, netted, and trapped in Virginia

Like tribal organization, religion was simple. There was a spirit, perhaps a god, called by a variant of Manitou or Manido. He was the owner of all things but he did not intervene in men's affairs. Almost everything in nature also belonged to a lesser spirit owner. Instead of priests, trained in ritual, the Algon- kians had shamans. Among some tribes, these shamans developed into remarkable magicians. They had such tricks as making the hut shake as if a terrible storm were blowing, making animal spirits talk out of the darkness, or plunging a knife into the air and bringing it back covered with blood.

53

Late 16th century engraving of an ancient, shamanistic type of Virginia ceremony

Passamaquoddy box of birchbark, made shortly after 1900

Bark container of the Algonquin tribe of eastern Canada

In the northern United States, the Algonkians dressed much as did the Iroquoians, and those living near the Atlantic Coast wore their hair in similar style, the men plucked or shaved, with a scalp lock, the women long-haired. Along the coast to the south, in Virginia and North Carolina, the people dressed like the Southeasterners. At the western end of the arc of hunting people were men with long hair, done in two braids, and farther north in the sub-Arctic, clothing was more finely tailored and fitted, after the manner of the Eskimos.

From Wisconsin east, the typical dwelling of the Algonkians was the wigwam. Because there is so much confusion about it, it is worth saying that a wigwam is entirely different from a tepee. It is a dome-shaped house, the frame made of strong poles planted in the earth and bent together, with others tied on crossways. It is covered with bark—preferably

Almost all aspects of Indian life are shown together in this 1590 picture of Secota, a Virginia Indian village

birchbark, where good birchbark could be had—or with rushes, or with mats woven from rushes, or with reeds. A small wigwam can be built quickly, but unlike a tepee, it cannot easily be taken apart, moved, and set up again. It is intended to stay put—and many wigwams were quite large.

Along the Atlantic Coast to the south, the Algonkians also built long, round-roofed houses, similar to those of the Iroquoians. A few tribes, such as the Abenakis, used a kind of tepee, in which straight poles were arranged to form a cone. Instead of covering the cone with skin, as in the common kind of tepee, bark was laid over the poles and held in position with more poles laid on top. This framework could easily be taken down and moved.

At the northern tip of the High Plains, the edge of the old range of the buffaloes in Canada, were the Crees, Algonkians who used the true tepee, a tent of skins neatly adapted to a mobile way of life.

Within the United States, the chief tribe that kept pretty much to the older, pre-farming way of life in historic times (that is, after white men arrived to make records and write history) were the Chippewas, who were strong north and south of Lake Michigan and Lake Superior, in Canada and in Wisconsin and Minnesota. Others, such as the Menominees and the Siouan-speaking Winnebagos of Wisconsin, were similar, but much less numerous.

The Chippewas did very little farming, but they fished on a tremendous scale. Their land could have been farmed, but having plenty of other food, more

The Chippewas of the Great Lakes region made wide use of birchbark; fish and wild rice were staples of their diet

easily come by, they planted only as a side line. Farming with primitive tools is hard work, and in the north, where the growing season is short, the yield may be too small to be worth the trouble. The two great lakes and countless smaller ones were full of fish, and the hunting was excellent. In addition, these people had a rich supply of a grain they did not have to cultivate at all—wild rice. It is still one of their most important crops.

The Chippewas were in good trapping country and furnished much of the fur that was traded at first through the Hurons to the French, later through the Iroquois to the British. As a result of this fur trade, they obtained European goods, including weapons, and with their superior weapons they became aggressive, pushing other tribes out of the rich, forested,

Birchbark canoes were light and easily carried from one lake to another during long voyages, as shown at left

Tepee-shaped bark wigwam of the Micmacs of Canada

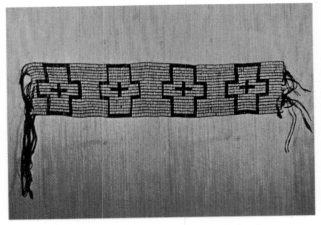

European influence is reflected in the Cree coat above. Its cut is derived from European models and steel needles were necessary for making it. The shoulder bag at left was collected among the Delawares, but was more likely made by the Creeks or Cherokees

The Delaware baby carrier ornament, below, has a primeval design that shows no trace of European influence

hunting country and away from the wonderful fishing of the lakes, to the south and west. Among the people they dislodged were the Dakota tribes, known to us as the Sioux, whom they drove out of the Woodlands into the Plains sometime around the beginning of the eighteenth century.

The beginnings of civilization that came into North America from Mexico in ancient times must have reached many of the Algonkians centuries before the white men came. Some of them, towards the west, must have had contact with the northern Mound Builders. Into this mass of related peoples came the invading Iroquoians, thrusting themselves northwards to the eastern Great Lakes and the Saint Lawrence River, even reaching into Canada. The Algonkians were then divided into three parts—the Woodland Hunters; the tribes west of the Iroquoians, mostly in Ohio and Illinois, who became the Western Farmers; and those east of the invaders, along the Atlantic Coast from Maine to North Carolina. This chapter deals with the hunters and the coastal people. Anthropologists often classify all three groups with the Iroquoians as a single cultural unit: the Eastern Woodlands. Certainly the Algonkians of the coast and the Iroquoians had much in common; in this book they are described in separate chapters because their origins and histories are so different.

The eastern Algonkians were farmers, and knew such arts as pottery-making and weaving, but on the whole, their products were not as fine as those of the Iroquoians and Southeasterners. Much of their pottery, in comparison to that of their neighbors, was coarse. They made one type of pottery, decorated by pressing string into the unbaked clay to make patterns, that seems to be traceable northwestwards,

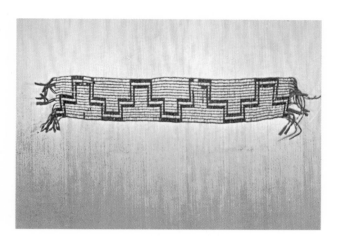

Another Penn wampum belt. The lines are thought to stand for rivers or mountains

Mohican shoulder bags. Such bags were first made in the south but spread north to the Great Lakes. Modeled on early bullet pouches, they served no purpose and were worn only on ceremonial occasions

through Canada and Alaska to an ancient, Siberian style. The knowledge of it, then, may have come, not from tribes influenced by Mexico, but from immigrants into the New World who learned the art in Asia.

The Algonkians who lived right on the coast developed one remarkable craft: the making of wampum from clamshells and certain other, thick shells. The tricky thing about wampum is the shaping of it. Even with primitive tools and no metal, it is not overly difficult to form beads by cutting shells into flat disks, rubbing them until they are round, and boring a hole in the middle. Necklaces of such shells are common today in the Southwest; they are usually called wampum, but they are not. Real wampum was made by cutting a longish strip of shell, sanding it down until it formed a smooth cylinder, and boring a hole the long way through the cylinder. To do this without splitting the bead, whether with a very fine stone drill or a wooden drill dipped in wet sand, was no small accomplishment, and wampum was correspondingly valuable. Since only a small part of a clamshell is purple, the purple beads were more valuable than the white.

The white men brought metal tools that made wampum-making easier, although still no child's play. The last chapter told how many uses the Iroquoians had for it; it was prized by many tribes, even to the distant Chippewas. With metal tools, the quantity of wampum increased. Inland tribes bought it for high prices in what goods they could offer—the Iroquoians also took it in tribute, or simply helped themselves.

A shortage of currency in both the early Dutch and English colonies led the colonists to use wampum as a substitute. Laws were passed fixing its value.

Aboriginal dress of Virginia chiefs or important warriors and (below) cooking succotash.
This was the original and quite savory dish that included fish as well as corn and beans

Some of the colonists started making it; then enterprising individuals took samples to Europe, where they were copied in porcelain and brought back to circulate as counterfeit. The counterfeit destroyed the value of the real article. To the Indians, the imitations were just as pretty as the originals, and just as suitable for decorative purposes—as well as being cheaper. Wampum disappeared, and to replace it there began the trade in beads with the Indians that lasted until this century.

The civilizing influences of the more advanced cultures brought a richer way of life to many of these northeastern tribes, but fruitful as such contacts may have been, they were also harassing. The stronger, better-organized nations, the Cherokees and Siouan peoples at the upper end of the true Southeastern culture, and the Iroquoians, pressed upon them, sometimes collected tribute from them, and kept them in a continuous state of warfare.

This pressure tended to make the loosely organized tribes unite more strongly and form larger groupings, and with this, chiefs became more powerful. By the time the French and English began settling among them, the eastern Algonkians were grouped in a series of loose confederacies, ranging from eight to as many as thirty villages; but most of these confederacies lacked the firm union of the Iroquois League.

The Algonkians were the people who received the first French and later the first English settlers, who taught them how to plant corn, bake clams, and how to bury a pot of beans overnight in a hole in which a fire had been made, so that the beans were baked the next morning. They taught them how to bake a corn cake that is still known by its Indian name, "pone." They taught the white men how to make canoes, to use seaweed for fertilizer, to eat pumpkins and squash, and to smoke tobacco. From the Algonkians we get such words as sachem, tomahawk, squaw, papoose, quahog, hominy, and succotash. The tribes welcomed the newcomers in friendship, and all along the coast, relations between whites and Indians began with friendly treaties. But these tribes were in a hopeless position.

Inland from them were the nations of the main stem of the culture from the south, far more powerful and more ferocious. The French, and above all the English, had not come simply to trade; they had come to occupy and work the land. The English were

The idea of annual ceremonies, like the dance below, came to Virginia from the Southeast

Powhatan in his royal wigwam, from a map of 1612

He gave the English—the "Yinglees," who were to become the "Yankees"—a very bad fright, and destroyed twelve settlements.

The colonists fought back with an equally savage form of total war. Massacre followed massacre; Indian women and children were slaughtered by the hundreds or burned alive in their wigwams along with their men, and the power of the New England Indians was broken. Philip was killed and his body hacked to bits; his wife and son were sold as slaves.

It was the Dutch who first took over what is now New York, beginning by settling on Manhattan Island. (There is some question whether their famous purchase of the Island for twenty dollars was made from Indians who lived there or from a passing band. If the second theory is correct, the equivalent of selling Brooklyn Bridge goes back a long time.)

The Dutch started the alliance with the Iroquois that the English inherited; on the Algonkians, they were just as hard as the others. Like the English, they often followed the pattern of attacking an unsuspecting and peaceful village in punishment for an offense committed by an entirely different tribe. After one particularly grim slaughter, when babies were hacked to death, some eighty Indian heads were placed in the streets of New Amsterdam, where the governor's wife played football with them.

"Powhatan's Mantle," a skin cloak decorated with shell, was brought back to England by some early explorer

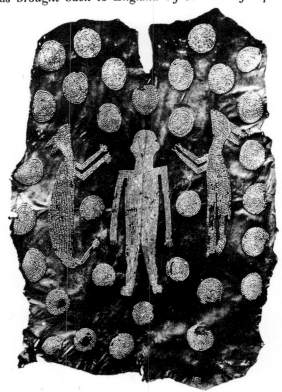

pouring across the ocean to form new and better versions of England. As their numbers increased, they needed more land. The Algonkians were between the hammer and the anvil.

The strongest Algonkian groups were the Powhatan Confederacy of Virginia—named for the chief who almost had John Smith executed—and the Delawares. In these tribes, the chiefs had Southeastern-style authority. The English called Powhatan "king," and recognized his authority by placing on his head a crown sent in the name of the king of England. His daughter married an Englishman and went to London. For a time all went well, but year by year his people were more tightly hemmed in, and Powhatan saw the writing on the wall. He attacked, the British retaliated, and Powhatan was crushed.

Massassoit, chief of the Wampanoags, received the Pilgrims with kindness and befriended the English until he died. His son, Metacomet, called King Philip, baptized, educated in the white man's schools, saw no hope for his people but to drive the white men back. He brought the powerful Narragansetts of Rhode Island, the Pequots of Connecticut, and other tribes into alliance with him and in 1675 rose in King Philip's War, which lasted two years.

Ætatis suæ 21. Aº. 1616.

Pocahontas
British School
National Gallery of Art
Washington, D.C.
(Mellon Collection)

Pocahontas, the daughter of Powhatan, the first Indian of noble rank to visit England. She went there with her English husband, John Rolfe, and her portrait was painted in London in 1616, when she was twenty-one. She died of smallpox in 1617

Portrait presumed to be Ninigret, sachem of one branch of the Narragansetts of Rhode Island in the early 17th century. He managed to keep his branch out of King Philip's War, and thus avoid having them massacred by the aroused colonists

The Great God who is the power and wisdom that made you and me Incline your hearts to Rightousness Love and peace. This I send to Assure you of my Love, and to desire your Love to my friends, and when the Great God brings me among you I Intend to order all things in such manner that we may all live in Love and peace one with another which I hope the Great God will Incline both me and you to do. I seek nothing but the honor of his name, and that we who are his workmanship, may do that which is well pleasing to him. The man which delivers this unto you, is my Special friend Sober wise and Loving, you may believe him. I have already taken care that none were of my people wrong you, by good Laws I have provided for that purpose, nor will I ever allow any of my people to sell Rumme to make your people drunk. If anything should be out of order, expect when I come, it shall be mended, and I will bring you some things of our Country that are useful and pleasing to you. So I rest In ye Love of our god yt made us I am

England 25 : 2 : 1682

I wrote this to the Indians
by an Interprs to the
6 mo 1682
Tho. Holme

your Loveing Freind
WM PENN

Penn's Treaty—the white man's version of the wampum belts shown on pages 58, 59

The French in Canada did make an alliance with the northern Algonkians, but this only meant that they fought with the French against the English and the Iroquois in a series of losing wars. Even their alliances ended in disaster for these Indians.

The Delawares were one of the strongest of the coastal tribes. William Penn made a famous treaty of peace with them when he founded Pennsylvania, and as long as Penn lived the treaty was kept. In 1720 they were one of the few non-Iroquoian tribes to accept the Iroquois' Great Peace with its humiliating terms. The Iroquois protected them for a time, then they moved west. The main body, seeking freedom at first—finally seeking only a home in which to be at peace—made treaties, settled, and was moved on again seven separate times, to end at last on the alien soil of Oklahoma. Other fragments wound up in Kansas, in Wisconsin, and in three places in Ontario.

What Indians confronted when they tried to be peaceful and progressive is horribly illustrated by the massacre at Gnadenhutten in Ohio, in 1782. Gnadenhutten was a settlement of Christian Delawares under Moravian missionaries. In order to avoid trouble with American frontiersmen, the Indians moved to the Moravian mission at Sandusky. They had planted crops in their home fields, however, so a number of them went back to the settlement to gather the harvest. There they were found by a party of about one hundred Americans under a militia colonel, David Williamson. The white men disarmed them, tied them up, then wiped them out with hand weapons—axes, tomahawks, and clubs—thus wasting no valuable ammunition. The Indians prayed and sang hymns. Thirty-five men, twenty-seven women, and thirty-four children were thus disposed of.

Most of the tribes that befriended the white men are extinct or exist as mere remnants. Some of the Abenakis of Maine found refuge in Canada, where they still are. In Maine, the Passamaquoddys and Penobscots still exist under state guardianship. There are scattered, little groups of people who consider themselves Indian in Massachusetts and Rhode Island, but the Narragansetts, who once occupied thirty villages and received tribute from other tribes, are now little more than a tradition. A few Mohicans and Pequots remain on tiny state reservations in Connecticut, and on Long Island are some groups on similar lands who claim Indian descent. In Virginia are the mixed-blood Chickahominys, Mattaponis, and Pamunkeys. In the mountains of North Carolina

Drum made by the Chippewas of the Great Lakes region

are several thousand poor farmers known as the Lumbees, having enough Indian descent to put them under the state's racial segregation laws. On the Indian side, they are probably a mixture of Algonkian and Siouan. They have no reservation, no tribal existence, virtually no Indian culture—nothing but a tradition, a number of disadvantages, and pride. In the same state, the eastern Cherokees occupy the federal Qualla Reservation.

Some of the western tribes, such as the Chippewas and Menominees, had better luck than their eastern relatives. The white men, pushing westward, at first grabbed only the best parts of an infinite land, bypassing tough tribes occupying less choice country. Poor though these tribes are today, much though they have suffered, they still exist as tribes and on reservations carved out of their native land.

French lithograph of 1842 showing a Menominee war dance. By this time, trade goods had reached these Indians as shown by the metal tomahawks and the woolen clothing

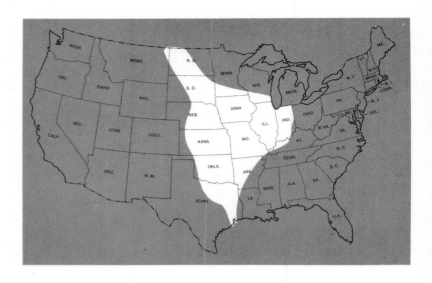

The Western Farmers

This chapter bites off a big mouthful. It deals with various tribes inhabiting a vast area reaching from just below the Canadian border to the northeastern edge of Texas. Students of Indian history often classify these tribes in several separate groups; many of the tribes are likely to be grouped with the Plains Indians to the west, while those tribes that lived in the northeast may be treated as a branch of the Eastern Woodland Indians.

In this vast region, the lines of division between cultures are fuzzy. The peoples of the Southeast formed a neat cultural unit. The East Coast Algonkians also formed a fairly neat unit, as did the Iroquoians. Now, as we move west, the different groups fade into one another, so a line of division between cultures, no matter where it is drawn, is bound to be somewhat arbitrary.

Beginning in the south, the land of the Western Farmers started in Texas where it blended into the southeast; from there, the area reached up through Arkansas and the eastern two-thirds of Oklahoma, up into part of Kansas and through Missouri, Iowa, and eastern Nebraska. One branch reached eastward across the Mississippi to occupy Illinois and Indiana

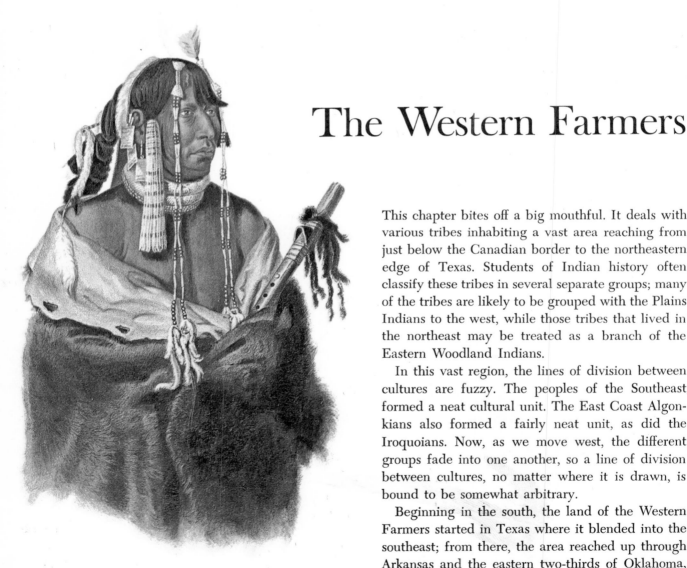

A young Mandan painted by Bodmer. He is painted and decked out in his most elaborate finery. Flutes, such as the one he is holding, were used mainly during courtship

"Pawnee Women Preserving Corn," painted by Alvin Jake, a modern Pawnee artist

south of the territory of the Woodland Hunters, and into Ohio up to the boundaries of the Iroquoian country. Another branch, bending northwestward with the Missouri River, reached to North Dakota and, in early times, as far west as eastern Montana.

The knowledge of farming came from Mexico into the Southeast, and from there spread east, north, and west. It continued moving westward until it came to a natural boundary that stopped farming—the line beyond which the annual rainfall averages less than twenty inches.

The map shows the line east of which an annual rainfall of twenty inches can safely be expected. West of this line, in the country known as the High Plains, the average drops rapidly to fifteen inches or less. *Average* annual rainfall is not a safe thing on which to plan a farming career. There are years when the rainfall on the High Plains is ample, well above the average, but too many others when it falls as low as four inches and, as white men have learned so painfully, farmers are scorched out. In prehistoric times, bands of farming Indians moved out into the grass country in periods of extra-heavy rainfall, but when the wet years ended they had the sense to pull back.

The zone of steady farming ended some distance behind the twenty-inch line, where a really dry year was a rarity.

Almost all the tribes mentioned in previous chapters were visited by white men of intelligence, education, and curiosity before the Indians' way of life had been influenced by white civilization. Now the story changes. Trade goods, metal tools, some weapons, and new ideas spread westward far ahead of the white men, changing the primitive cultures. The horse —the greatest of the Europeans' contributions to Indian culture—reached the western tribes well before the Europeans themselves. Everywhere, as the white men dislocated and drove out tribes along the coast, migrations and invasions resulted, creating confusions, bringing new influences, stirring up the mixture.

Many of the first white men to visit the Western Farmers were traders and hunters who were almost or entirely illiterate, who brought about great changes without being able to describe, or caring to describe, how the tribes lived before these foreign influences were introduced. The best descriptions of unchanged tribes come from French missionary-explorers, and these are all too few. We depend largely on the finds of archaeologists to tell us how people lived in the area even as late as the 1600's.

In general, we know that this area was once occupied by people who did considerable farming and also hunted; that most of them hunted buffalo on the prairies and the High Plains to the west; that they lived in large, settled villages, made pottery, and seemed to be pretty well off. Some of them made finer pottery, farmed on a larger scale, and moved about less than did their descendants of more recent times.

The northeastern, Indiana-Illinois branch of the area when it was first visited by white men, was occupied by the Sauk and Fox (a single tribe), Illinois, Kickapoos, Shawnees, and Miamis—all Algonkian tribes. They were probably newcomers who had been pushed west by the Iroquoians or south by such Woodland tribes as the Chippewas. These stronger tribes, in driving the weaker Algonkians away from the rich hunting and fishing along the Great Lakes, had no idea that they were pushing them into some of the finest farming land in North America.

When the Algonkians moved into this section, they found a situation somewhat like that of their relatives on the East Coast—they were in a position to be heavily influenced by the Iroquoians and Southeasterners,

Pottery of the Mandan and Hidatsa. The slightly squared necks and incised decorations on the two outside pots suggest the style of pottery made by the Iroquoians

and also to be constantly troubled by them. The influence of new ideas and customs was strengthened in historic times by the arrival of the Delawares, who began on the shores of the Atlantic, where they were much affected by Southeastern culture.

The Shawnees also came out of the east, but before the time of the white men. They seem to have been a nation that liked to travel. For a time one branch went south and lived among the Creeks, with whom they formed a friendship. Later, one part of the tribe

Contact with the white men—Hidatsas at a fortified post in 1834 painted by Bodmer. Prince Maximilian of Wied has his hand inside his coat; beside him stands the artist

Pawnee village. This painting was taken from a photograph made in 1871 in Nebraska

settled in Ohio, another in southern Illinois—believing, like the Delawares, that they had found a rich land in which they could live in peace.

The culture of the western, farming Algonkians was in a transition between that of the old, hunting tribes of the Woodlands and the tribes of the Southeast. Early white visitors to the tribal lands tell of the Indians' cornfields stretching for miles along the river valleys, and their large villages of comfortable, solid wigwams. Since this was not birchbark country, the wigwams were covered with mats, and the canoes were hollowed out of large logs, Southeastern style. These canoes were too heavy for portages, and were used only on the waters on which they were launched; for journeys beyond their local watersheds the people went on foot, the men carrying the arms, the women carrying the packs.

West of the Mississippi were many powerful tribes, among them the Caddos in northeast Texas, from whom the Caddoan family of languages takes its name. Other Caddoan tribes in the area were the Wichitas in Kansas, the Pawnees in Nebraska, and the Arikaras in North Dakota. These tribes had unquestionably moved out of the Southeast; the Caddos

themselves could as well be classed Southeastern as Western Farmer. There was also an important Algonkian farming tribe west of the Mississippi, the Cheyennes, who lived somewhat east of central North Dakota. Their way of life, however, seems to have been closer to that of the Mandan and Hidatsa—both Siouan tribes—than to any of the other Algonkians.

The rest of the area was occupied by tribes of the Siouan family. The family gets its name from the Sioux, whom we know as the greatest of the tepee-dwelling, buffalo-hunting, horseback-riding, nomadic, warrior tribes—but in those days there were no horses in the New World, the Plains Indians as we think of them today did not exist, and the Sioux, later so great, were simply a group of closely related Woodland Hunters living west of the Chippewas. Some of them did a little farming, and from time to time they went into the High Plains to kill a few buffalo. Other Siouan tribes—notably the Mandan, the Omaha, and the Osage—were people of far more advanced culture.

West of the Mississippi, from Arkansas north were, among others, the Ponca, Oto, Osage, Omaha, Missouri, Kansa, Iowa, Mandan, and Hidatsa. These

69

were people of power. Between their fields, the local hunting, and the buffalo, they lived well. They were energetic people; the impression we get from early descriptions is of exuberance, of people who are going places.

Not much is known of the early history of the farming Siouans. They were not merely *influenced* by the Southeast, but were *carriers* of a culture that probably derived from the early Mound Builders. We find Siouans at the western end of the wooded country along the Canadian border with a hunting culture. We find them on the Gulf Coast with a full Southeastern culture. The Mandan and Hidatsa have the tradition of having come from the east, up the Missouri River, into North Dakota. They unquestionably brought farming with them. Did the main body of Siouans once occupy the Southeast and Ohio and then get driven out, leaving some tribes behind? Or did some invade the Southeast and stay there?

It seems strange that the quite powerful Siouan tribes did not occupy and hold the rich lands of Indiana, Illinois, and Ohio; from what we know of them, they do not seem like a people the Algonkians could have driven out. Nor do we know why the

Caddoan Arikara, who were such great farmers that the sign for them in the old Indian sign language was the motion of grinding corn, should have traveled all the way to North Dakota from their original homeland. What we don't know about these tribes, in fact, would fill a book.

In moving so far north, the cornplanters accomplished something that would be a credit to modern agronomists. Farther south they raised tall corn that required a long growing season. On the northern prairies, they developed a short corn that would mature more quickly and with somewhat less rain. But then, one of the marvels of Indian corn is the way it was adapted to so many different climates. About all that white men have done with it since has been to improve the innumerable varieties the Indians developed; in recent times, some advanced breeders of hybrid corn have gone back to the Indians for backcrosses to restore some of the aboriginal hardiness.

Farming tribes were established west of the Mississippi and out over the well-watered prairies by 1300. From early times, the type of house they built was the earth lodge, which remained the standard dwelling for Indians from Nebraska north. This was

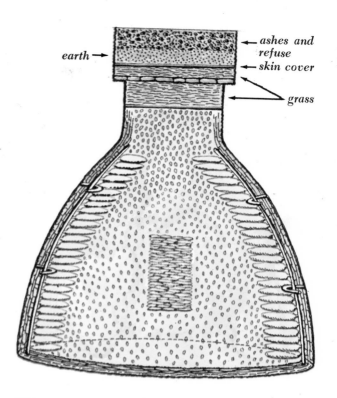

earth →
← ashes and refuse
← skin cover
grass

Hidatsa storage pit for crops. The cover of ashes and refuse was intended to camouflage the pit from enemies

Harvest time in a Pawnee village. The Pawnees lived in Nebraska; in summer, the whole tribe would go out on the Plains to hunt buffalo, to return to their villages in time for the harvest

Catlin's painting of a Mandan village curiously does not show the vestibules leading to the entrances of the earth lodges that are usually considered typical of these lodges

a solid structure of rafters carried on a strong central framework. The wall and roof rafters (the walls sloped inward and were part wall, part roof) were covered with willow branches; over these was placed grass, then sod, and finally a layer of earth. The whole dwelling might have had grass laid over it, sometimes tied in bundles. Many lodges were strong enough for people to gather on the roofs in good weather.

A form of vestibule was built extending from the entrance to the main part of the lodge. The central part of the lodge floor was often dug out to a shallow depth, which increased the height to the ceiling and provided a bench around the outer edge; in a good-sized Pawnee lodge, a hundred people could easily find seats on this bench. A square opening was left in the roof, under which a fire was built. The height from the floor to the ceiling was around eleven feet; floor measurements of forty to forty-five square feet were common, and lodges built for ceremonial purposes were considerably larger.

The basic idea of a dwelling partly dug into the ground, with a vestibule entrance and a central smoke hole, is extremely old and widespread. It is the pattern of the Eskimo igloo, of the kiva of the Southwest, and is also found in Siberia.

The layout of smoke hole and door, with no windows, suggests a stuffy, airless dwelling, and probably in the dead of winter, when the door was tightly closed with hides, the air got pretty thick as well as warm, but so long as even a slight draft was allowed through the doorway the ventilation system was good. A constant current moved through the vestibule to the fire, where, being warmed, it rose through the smoke hole. The outgoing warm air drew in more fresh air.

Often the villages were fortified, either with stockades of poles or with earthen ramparts as tall as six feet. Many villages were placed on bluffs overlooking rivers, in locations that could be approached from one direction only. Fortifications of this sort are found

Hidatsa village on the banks of the Missouri. The artist, Catlin, shows Indians bathing in the river and playing along its banks, and himself and his companions being ferried across it in a bullboat made of buffalo hide

The remains of an Arikara earth lodge close to the mouth of the Cheyenne River in South Dakota. This lodge was occupied between 1750 and 1790. The hole in the front right-hand corner served as a storage pit in which the lodge's inhabitants stored their grain and other crops

Interior of a Mandan lodge as painted by Bodmer in the 1830's. Favorite horses are stabled inside the lodge, and assorted gear hangs from the supporting poles

among prehistoric villages excavated by archaeologists, but they were probably more widespread after the Indians obtained horses, which resulted in something of an increase in raiding.

Another basic type of dwelling, the grass lodge, probably came up from the prehistoric Southeast, as it was most common among Caddoan tribes. In this, poles were driven in a circle in the ground and bent together at the top. The result was a curved cone, not a round dome as in a wigwam. Lighter poles were lashed horizontally around this framework, and to them was tied a thick thatch of grass. The finished product was roomy and solid and looked rather like an enormous, shaggy beehive.

The houses built by the Osages, a Siouan tribe living in southern Missouri and northern Arkansas, were oval or rectangular and had straight walls and curved roofs covered with mats or skins. (Being within striking distance of the buffalo, the Osages had a good supply of heavy skins.) These buildings ran from thirty to one hundred feet in length, fifteen to twenty feet in width, and were, on the average, ten feet high. There is a suggestion here of the Iroquoian longhouse, but we have no knowledge as yet of any contact between the two peoples.

From Siberia into Alaska, and on down to the land of the Western Farmers, there were tents built on the smoke-hole principle. A framework of three or four poles, lashed together near the top or hooked together by interlocking crotches, was set up, with the lower ends well apart. More poles were laid against this, their bottom ends forming a circle. Over the whole, skins were stretched in such a way as to leave an opening at the top. This was the primitive form of the tepee. A person could, and still can, have a fire in a tepee without being smoked out.

The tents of white men are, typically, closed at the top. Since early times we have had the A-tent and the pyramid tent; in the Middle Ages, knights and nobles had handsome, large, round tents with pointed roofs. You could not have a wood fire in any of them without making yourself perfectly miserable.

The tepee was probably invented in the Arctic to keep out the cold, but it is also a good tent in hot weather, when our tents, under direct sun, become intolerable. The arrangement allows lifting a section of the tent at the bottom, and again the principle of air movement comes into play. Air heated by the sun striking the sides of the tent rises through the smoke hole; cooler air flows in along the ground.

Modern reproductions of Wichita grass houses, built at "Indian City," Anadarko, Oklahoma. The one at right is unfinished. The Caddo also built similar houses

The farming tribes used their tepees mostly when they went out after buffalo. As a rule, this was an annual affair when the great herds, in their migrations, came nearest to tribal territory.

Hunting the big, thick-hided buffalo was not an easy business for a man on foot, armed with a stone-tipped lance and stone-tipped arrows, and could be fatally dangerous if a bull turned on him or a herd stampeded over him. The tepees then were small because the poles had to be dragged along by dogs. They were cumbersome things to carry about because of the number of poles required, but they were quickly set up and quickly struck. On the hunt, the people went on foot, always with one eye peeled for another tribe with whom they might not be on friendly terms and who might be after the same herd.

Much of the hunting was done by stampeding the animals; for example, by setting fire to the grass and driving the buffalo either over a cliff or past a line of archers who picked off as many as they could. The kill was limited by what could be eaten on the spot, plus what could be dried, or "jerked," and carried back for later use. The amount of meat and the number of hides that could be carried was what the women could take on their backs, or what could be

Omaha village of 1850 with tepees and earth lodge

Buffalo were sometimes taken by driving them into a corral, after which they could be killed with bows and arrows. Above, Catlin shows hunters disguised in wolfskins

The Mandans' dogs helped earn their keep by pulling toboggans on winter travels

added—which was not much—to the burdens already dragged by the dogs. The Indians had no wheels, no wagons. Instead, they made a contraption known as a travois. Two tepee poles were tied to the shoulders of a dog, the free ends dragging on the ground, and across these the load was placed. In winter, the northern tribes used toboggans, on which heavier loads could be hauled, but during the winters the buffalo were in the south.

Much as they wanted the meat, the warm robes, and the useful skins, the women must have looked forward to the big hunt with some dread, for their position was a hard one. At home their position was better, for they were the mistresses of the fields, and the crops belonged to them. Farming meant a lot of work for the women, but it left them some leisure, and it gave them authority. It was also a demonstration of woman's mystic power—the gift of fertility, of creating life.

Throughout the area are found signs of a cultural relationship with the Southeast. Most tribes had clans, some of which traced descent through the mother, some through the father. Many clans were also divided into halves, or moieties, as with the Iroquois, Creek, and Natchez; others arranged their clans into several larger groups. As a rule, the members of a clan, even though they might come from different villages and be total strangers, were regarded as relatives who helped each other and, as

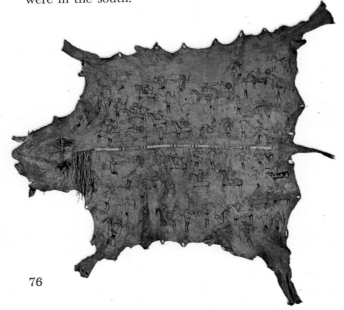

The Mandan buffalo robe at left is the oldest painted buffalo hide in existence. It records an attack made by Sioux and Arikara warriors on the Mandan tribe in 1797

76

Dance of the Mandan Female White Buffalo Society, as seen in the 1830's by Bodmer

Mandan bullboats were made by stretching buffalo hides over a frame of light wood

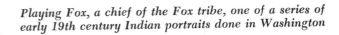
often left the medical treatment to specialists in medicine. Among some tribes, there were true priests, who presided over ceremonies that required those who officiated to have priestly training.

Partly through the visions of inspired individuals, partly by ways now lost in the mist of antiquity, there sprang up among the Western Farmers a collection of sacred objects, such as the sacred arrows of the Cheyennes, or, more often, what are called "medicine bundles" or "sacred bundles."

The white men saw that the Indians combined healing with religion—as did white men until not so long ago—so they called all Indian religious practitioners "medicine men." They saw that the Indians wrapped objects they considered sacred in various

relatives, could not intermarry. Such clans are called "exogamous," meaning "outward marrying." A lesser number of clans were "endogamous"; members married only within the clan.

Chieftainships were well defined. Among some tribes, chiefs were appointed, among others the rule was handed down within certain families. Many tribes, especially in the northeastern area, had both war and peace chiefs, the peace chiefs being the actual governors, the war chiefs the leaders of war parties. When the Shawnee leader Tecumseh formed the great Algonkian alliance against the United States, he stressed the fact that "the chiefs," meaning the peaceful governors, were no longer in charge.

Visions were important in religion. Young men went in search of them, usually going off by themselves and praying for a supernatural visitor. The vision a young man might receive was an indication of the extent to which he had acquired special strength from the all-pervading, unseeable god. Very strong visions led a man to become a shaman, in which case he read the future, gave news of people at a distance, and diagnosed illnesses—although he

Mato-Tope, a Mandan chief, in a shirt of mountain sheep hide. The same chief, in full paint, is shown on page 84

Elk's Horns, or Masheena, a sub-chief of the Kickapoos, painted by Catlin in 1831. He is praying while reading a "prayer stick," like the one at left. The symbols on the stick suggest the first steps toward a system of writing

kinds of bundles, often beautifully decorated. When white men were allowed to see what the objects were, they did not think much of them, any more than an Indian would think much of some of our sacred symbols. They saw that these bundles, or their contents, were sometimes used to heal the sick, just as, in the 1500's, the Spanish explorer Cabeza de Vaca treated sick Indians by touching them with a cross, so they called them "medicine bundles." This is as much as if Indians, seeing Christians pray for health were to call the cross "medicine sticks," and about as accurate.

The best name we have for these packages is "sacred bundles," and it will have to do. Many were personal property, handed down from father to son, or buried with the owner; others became clan or tribal property. Major rituals centered around them. The keeper of the bundle was instructed by the man from whom he had inherited it in the prayers and rites that went with it.

The northern tribes, both east and west of the Mississippi, gave reverence to the sacred pipe, or calumet. Pipes were carried in special dances, served as passports for messengers, and were used in many rituals. A pipe dressed with red feathers signified war; one with white feathers meant peace.

The bowl of a true calumet was made from a stone called catlinite, found in Minnesota. This stone is soft and easy to work when first dug out of the ground, but later hardens. The bowl of the pipe was fitted with a long stem which was elaborately decorated. Some pipes were smoked only on ceremonial occasions, in which case tobacco that was raised with special ritual by the men was used. Others were smoked for pleasure, using ordinary tobacco.

The special reverence for smoking and tobacco, and for the pipes themselves, seems to be a pattern that developed spontaneously among the Farmers and does not derive from the cultures farther east.

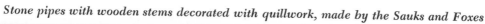

Stone pipes with wooden stems decorated with quillwork, made by the Sauks and Foxes

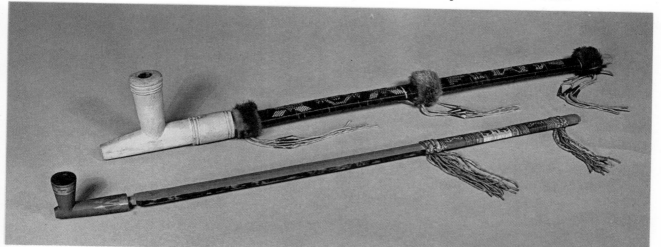

Catlin's painting of the climax of the four-day religious ordeal in which young Mandan warriors voluntarily went through tortures to prove their courage and their fortitude

Some of the religious customs and ceremonies showed strong Southeastern influence and some even had Aztec overtones. The Pawnees, for example, had a definite sun worship and related star cult, including an annual Morning Star ceremony. At this ceremony, a captured maiden was sacrificed. The captive might have been taken at any time during the year. She was well treated, and told nothing of her fate. Three days before the great day, she was stripped of her clothing, painted all over, and treated as a sacred person. Every attempt was made to keep her from divining her fate.

Before the morning star rose on the fourth day, she was led to a raised scaffold. It was considered a lucky sign if, in her innocence, the girl mounted the scaffold without resistance. Then she was tied. Priests symbolized torture of her, but did not actually hurt her. Then, just as the morning star rose, a man shot her in the body from in front; at the same moment, another struck her over the head with a club. Death was instantaneous. Her heart was cut out as a sacri-

fice to the star, and every male in the tribe shot an arrow into her body, older relatives doing this in the name of boys too young to draw a bow themselves.

Early in the nineteenth century, a young Pawnee warrior of high reputation rebelled against this rite. At the critical moment, he cut the girl free from the scaffold, threw her on his horse, and ran off with her. He set her free near her own tribe. When he returned, he was not punished, but admired for his courage. The people seem to have been relieved to drop a cruel practice, and it ended there.

The symbolized torture clearly derives from the Southeast. Treating the victim as holy, holding the rite when a certain star appears at a certain time of the year, cutting out the heart, and many other details seem pure Aztec—except that the Aztecs would have sacrificed a man instead of a maiden.

In the Southeast, war achievement was the common man's road to fame and rank. It was a murderous business of wholesale killing and bringing home the gory samples as evidence, with the alternative of capturing a strong man to torture. Among the Western Farmers, except in the southern area where Southeastern influence was strongest, torture was not a requirement of war, and nowhere was it as hideous as farther east. The main thing was for a man to prove his courage, and the Western tribes believed that the greatest courage a man could show was to lay his bare hand upon an armed enemy, preferably one who was surrounded by his comrades. Killing from ambush was not honored; killing of any kind, in fact, was secondary to proving bravery, except on those rare occasions when tribes found it necessary to engage in serious war with each other. Scalps were usually taken, but they were not essential, and a man was not judged by the number he had.

The men danced before starting on a war party to get into the spirit of the thing and acquire power; after the skirmish, they danced again to celebrate the victory. The dance after a successful raid came to be called a "scalp dance," since any scalps taken were featured. In these dances, each warrior dramatized, in stylized form, what he would do or had done, bending low to track the enemy, leaping to the attack, going through the motions of combat. The footwork was light and quick, in time to fast,

A Dog Society dancer of the Hidatsa tribe in 1834

Mandan buffalo dance. Such rituals, with dancers portraying both hunters and game, were common all over the world, and were meant to give the hunters power over their quarry

more serious business. Hunting parties were carefully organized; often hunters were not allowed to go out without permission of the chief, in order that no hasty individual frighten away the game. This control was especially tight on the buffalo hunts. It could also apply to the distribution of the kill.

Among the Western Farmers we begin to find Indians who look as most people nowadays expect Indians to look. The comb of natural hair, made by shaving all the head except for a strip along the crown, was elaborated with an artificial brush, or roach, of deer's tail hairs, dyed red, to which feathers might be added to signify that the wearer had won

cheerful songs almost always attractive and sometimes beautiful, and to the rapid beat of a high-toned drum. It was a fine means of showing off.

Similar dances were performed for pure fun. Each individual danced as he pleased, so no rehearsal was necessary; one needed only to know the tune and how to dance. From these dances evolved the "war dances" that are now part of the commercial stock of Indians all over the United States.

Boasting was an important part of the war complex. On appropriate occasions, warriors stood up before their fellow tribesmen to recite their brave deeds. The performance was far from modest, but it had to be accurate; everyone kept careful track, and knew just what any man had a right to claim. If he claimed an act that was not his due, he would be hooted down and disgraced. White frontiersmen mixed this trait with whiskey and imagination to produce the famous "brags" of the early frontier.

Fighting was pretty much a sporting proposition, carried out by individual initiative. Hunting was a

An Omaha warrior reports to Young Elk, one of the chiefs of the tribe, in an 1851 sketch by Kurz. The chief is simply dressed as was usual except on special occasions

certain combat honors. Tribes that wore their hair long tied on these handsome roaches, too. Among some tribes, feathers were tied directly in the hair, standing up, lying flat, or hanging down, as badges of war achievement. Early portrayals of Omahas and some of the northernmost tribes even show "war bonnets" quite like those that are now so familiar.

The Western Farmers wore elaborate buckskin clothing often decorated with porcupine quill embroidery or, later, with beads. The general effect was similar to that which the Plains Indians later made famous, which is not surprising, since much of the Plains Indian culture derived from the Farmers.

The roach of deer's tail hairs was a common type of headpiece. The example below was made by the Sioux

Tenkswatawa, the Shawnee prophet who provided the religious force behind his brother Tecumseh's uprising

In the eighteenth century, horses that had run loose from the Spanish herds in New Mexico and increased fantastically on the good grazing of the Plains reached the Farmers, who soon learned to ride. With horses, both war and hunting became easier and more fun. The big hunts were much more comfortable, the women's part in them was greatly lightened. It was a break for the dogs, too. The Indians tended to stay on the hunt longer, live a somewhat shorter part of the year in the villages, and depend a little less upon the crops. At the time that horses came from the west, trade goods began coming from the east. While it lasted, the Western Farmers' way of life was richer than it had ever been.

The land occupied by these tribes included the areas that white men, seeking for farms, would most covet. It was impossible for the few thousand Indians to stand against the growing United States.

Like their eastern relatives, the western Algonkians found themselves between the British and French. They, too, tended to form alliances with the French, which, when Canada fell, turned out to be a mistake. Then they put their faith in the British,

who proceeded to lose first the Revolution, then the War of 1812. The Indians were left to face the Americans, from whom the French and British kings had shielded them; they found little mercy.

It was among the Algonkians that the two most ambitious attempts to form large confederacies against the whites occurred. The first was organized by Pontiac, an Ottawa, in the middle of the eighteenth century, threatened for a while, then died out. The second, and much more menacing, was led by the Shawnee Tecumseh against the Americans at the time of the War of 1812. Tecumseh was one of the noblest of Indian leaders, a statesman and great orator, a stern war leader, and yet a man of mercy who would not allow prisoners to be killed. More than one white family, seeing his warriors overrunning their land, found safety in his hands.

Tecumseh traveled from Illinois to the towns of the Creeks in the deep South, to the Osages, and to the Chippewas in an effort to enlist tribes in his confederacy. But his plan involved forgetting too many tribal feuds and making alliances with too many alien peoples. His confederacy was never strong enough, and when he himself was killed in the British retreat from Detroit, the uprising ended.

Mato-Tope, a Mandan chief

The Algonkians were debauched with liquor, first by French and then by English traders, then by the Americans, who used a barrel of whiskey as the standard prelude to a profitable treaty. The European kings, and to a lesser extent the republican government in Washington, tried to keep the treaties, but the frontiersmen would have none of it. Seldom were peaceful Indians so freely shot down in cold blood, promises so regularly broken, the doctrine that the only good Indian is a dead one so heartlessly put into practice. The deer and turkeys were killed off, the good farming lands taken. Weakened by drunkenness, poverty-stricken, hungry, broken, the tribes could no longer resist. Chief Black Hawk of the Sauks and Foxes made a futile attempt to hold onto his land in the pathetic, so-called "Black Hawk's War," and with that the resistance ended. Those Algonkian tribes that survive at all survive for the most part on bleak little holdings in Oklahoma.

The tribes west of the Mississippi fared somewhat better, although far from well. Smallpox was one of the white men's most devastating contributions to Indian life all over the continent. As the disease had never existed in the New World, its ravages, when it caught hold, were terrible. The western epidemic of 1837 broke the powerful Mandan and Hidatsa tribes, reducing the Mandans from 1,600 souls to 150, and doing just about as well by their neighbors.

The white men flowed around the farming Indians, surrounded them, engulfed them. By the middle of the nineteenth century, the policy had been adopted of concentrating as many Indians as possible in the "Indian Territory," which later became Oklahoma. The majority of the tribes mentioned in this chapter wound up there, regardless of original treaties, of whether they had put up a stiff fight or, like the Pawnees, decided that their day was done and that the only course was to keep the peace and try to learn from their conquerors.

The purpose of crowding Indians into Indian Territory was to place them on land that nobody wanted. Not until the United States began to fill up from coast to coast did white men begin to hunger after that poorer soil. Ironically, a few tribes found themselves sitting on mineral wealth. The greatest joke the white man ever played on himself was when he put the Osages, by force of arms, on undesirable

Catlin's portrait of the Bloody Hand, chief of the Arikaras. His face has been painted with vermilion earth

land under which was hidden one of the richest oil deposits on the continent of North America.

The remnants of the Mandan, Hidatsa, and Arikara tribes are in Montana. They have made a partial comeback since the great smallpox epidemic, numbering about 1,700 for all three tribes, or less than one-fifth their population at the height of their power. Their present holdings are not in territory suited to farming, and as the heart of their reservation, at Fort Berthold, was recently flooded by one of the new dams across the Missouri, it is difficult to see where they will turn next.

Medicine drum decorated with beads. It was made by the Osages and was used on ritual and ceremonial occasions

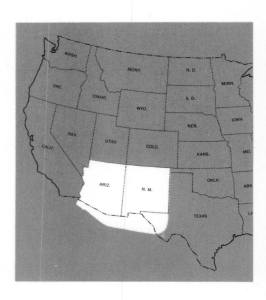

Dolls representing Kachinas, or sacred beings, are given to children as part of their religious education; at right is a Hopi Cactus Kachina doll

The Old Settlers

To-Pove, Pueblo painter, shows women bringing food to the men cleaning the irrigation ditch for their fields

In 1540 the Spanish explorer Coronado marched north from Mexico City, looking for the fabled Seven Cities of Gold. He passed first through the outer part of the Aztec empire, through cities and towns where the common people lived no more poorly than did those of Spain. He crossed the arid stretch lying along what is now the U.S.-Mexican border where he encountered small bands of poor and primitive desert rovers. Then, in the drainage of the upper Rio Grande, he came again to towns and villages where the people were well organized under strong governments. Their houses were arranged as compactly as in a medieval town, and many of their fields were irrigated. He had entered the eastern portion of what today we call the Southwest. He called the settlements of this region *pueblos*, which is Spanish for "towns." The name is still used today both for the towns and the people who live in them.

Drawn by the tales of the incredible wealth of the Seven Cities, he turned east and went on across the

A land no one would pick as a center of farming—Monument Valley in northern Arizona

High Plains, where he found people living in skin tents who followed the "wild cows." Finally, when he came to the grass lodges of the Wichitas, he gave up in despair and turned back.

The land in which the Pueblos settled, now Arizona and New Mexico, is sharply unlike the flat country of Texas and Oklahoma to the east or the howling deserts and coastal ranges of California to the west. It is a land of low rainfall, the greater part of it having less than the critical average of twenty inches a year. Its lowest parts, in the south, are two thousand feet or better above sea level except along the banks of the Colorado River; much of the area lies above five thousand feet, and in the north its highest peaks top thirteen thousand feet.

It is rugged country, seamed with canyons, and studded with flat-topped hills called mesas. It is strung with mountain ranges, the upper slopes of which are green and well watered. But these slopes are too high and have too short a growing season for farming. Rivers are few but water courses, or arroyos, are common. Violent floods occur in them after a rain; at other times they are dry. Over large parts of the Southwest, the midsummers are searingly hot, the winters fierce with cutting, icy winds and driving snow.

This is not the land anyone would pick as the place where there was the greatest dedication to agriculture in North America. Yet in this country, men made their principal living by farming unirrigated land, despite an average annual rainfall of only thirteen inches. In doing so, they showed a skill at dry farming and developing specialized varieties of corn that we, with all our technology, have never equalled.

In a country where big game was relatively scarce, the people relied on farming as their primary food source. From the civilizations to the south, they borrowed and developed squashes, tobacco, cotton, six colors of corn, and a number of kinds of beans. The dry farms called for endless labor. Where irri-

gation was developed, as it was wherever there was water for it, it brought with it much heavy work. Farming became a man's occupation, which is one of the two major differences between these people and other farming tribes such as the Southeasterners. The women stayed home, with time to elaborate and beautify their basketry and, above all, their pottery.

The second major difference between these people and the Southeasterners was that in the Southwest there was no human sacrifice or torture and a general dislike for war. Except among the Athabascan invaders and certain tribes along the Colorado River, a man got mighty little advancement out of being a

Hopi woman weaving a basket. Brightly colored, light and strong baskets are one of the Hopis' specialties

Among most of the settled tribes, religion was formalized, with rituals at fixed times of year. The myths on which the rituals were based, prayers, songs, all the elements of the dances, had to be exactly memorized. This, too, was largely men's work. From it developed a true art of music and dance-drama which used up much of the energy that Indians of other regions spent in war.

This kind of ritual required trained priests. Among some tribes, only a man of a certain descent could succeed a given priest. In the last few years the death or conversion to Christianity of certain Hopi Indians, with no one eligible to replace them, has put an end to several important ceremonies.

Among other tribes, a young man could enter upon priestly training if he was accepted by the priest or by the society that handled a specific ritual. Not every man was accepted. Usually, when a priest died, there would be one trainee who had reached the point where he could take over the ceremony, and through this succession, he might eventually become one of the governors of the tribe.

Even today, among some of the Pueblo tribes, it would be difficult to make up a strong war party without including at least some of the young men of the group described. If they were killed off, there might be no one to replace them.

It is a fact that anyone with rich possessions and stores of food who is surrounded by people with few possessions and little food is going to have to

warrior. The big battle was against the environment —to maintain a way of life of considerable richness, which required an assured food supply. War was a distraction, a diversion of energy from a productive purpose to a sterile one. It meant the loss of strong backs and arms that could ill be spared.

War could also result in a loss of knowledge as important as physical strength. Against the odds they faced, the greatest human force and human ingenuity by themselves were not enough to ensure crops. In such a battle, men need divine help. The religions came to center upon rain, the crops, and, as a result of these, upon the welfare of the people.

Pueblo jar. The Denver Art Museum identifies it as from Acoma, although the bird looks more like Zia work

fight, no matter how much he dislikes it. This was true in the Southwest. As a result there were war organizations and rituals, and some tribes had war societies and war priests. Many of them fought well. The Papagos and Pimas, in southern Arizona, were noted for their success against the Apaches, and all these Indians could be prickly customers on occasion, even the Hopis whose very name means "peaceful."

Necessary fighting was often surrounded by heavy ritual. Scalps, or in place of them a few strands of hair, were occasionally taken. Sometimes only certain men, of near-priestly standing, took scalps. These trophies were likely to be regarded with considerable fear and had to be purified, prayed over, and "fed" with offerings such as corn meal and pollen, to keep them harmless. The warrior who had killed someone had to go through elaborate purifications before he could rejoin his people. To do well in battle thus was a nuisance. The Pimas and Papagos required sixteen days of purification for a killer, which greatly limited their otherwise important value as allies to the U.S. Army against the Apaches. The Papagos designated only a few men out of a war party, men with special power from their visions, to do the killing if all went well. War was rationalized to fit the eternal quest for rain and fertility. Victory would capture the rain; the strength taken from the enemy would bring water.

In the area there are several tribes speaking languages of the big Uto-Aztecan family. The name comes from the fact that both the Utes of Utah and Colorado and the Aztecs of Mexico belong to it. The most important of these tribes in the Southwest are the Pimas and Papagos, who together make up the Pimans, in the southern part of Arizona and in northern Mexico, and the Hopis in northern Arizona. Along the Colorado River are the Yumans, a totally different linguistic group. Among the Pueblos, in addition to the Uto-Aztecan Hopis, are no less than three separate families with a number of languages: the Zuñi, near the Arizona border, and, farther east and in the Rio Grande valley, the Keresans and the Tanoans. Of these, the only ones having any near relationship to any speech outside the area are the Tanoans, whose language is related to Kiowa, spoken by a powerful Plains tribe. Scattered over New Mexico and Arizona are the tribes speaking Athabascan languages: the Navahos and Apaches, comparative newcomers.

Nowhere in America does one have a greater feeling of antiquity than in the Southwest. Everywhere the ancient arts, costumes, ways of speech, crafts, houses are preserved well enough to be recognizable. Here is antiquity on the hoof. It is probable that the Pimas and Papagos descend, at least in part, from the ancient Hohokam people who, in turn, derive from

San Xavier del Bac, built by Piman labor under Jesuit direction in the early 18th century

The Hopi pueblo of Walpi is built of stone; adobe, as at San Ildefonso and Acoma, came in later

the yet older Cochise culture. The Pueblos, or some of them, beyond doubt once inhabited the ruins that stare so picturesquely from the cliffs of the north, and to this day they practice rituals that were familiar to their ancestors a thousand years ago. Even the recent invaders, the Athabascans, have been in the country for nigh onto a thousand years; the first white men, the Spaniards, arrived in the late fifteen hundreds.

The old, settled, farming tribes of the Southwest fall into three cultural groups: the Pimans of southern Arizona; the Yumans along the Colorado River on the Arizona-California border; and the Pueblos.

The Pimas, from whom the Pimans take their name, lived along the Gila River, the only important stream in southern Arizona. They irrigated on a large scale, digging ditches many miles long with their primitive tools, raising food plants and cotton. South of them, extending into Mexico, were their close relatives the Papagos, called the "bean people" because in their extremely arid country they could raise beans better than anything else.

Papago house. The partly enclosed shelter provides a fine, cool place for daily life, protected from the sun

The Papago territory is a hard, unlikely piece of land in which to imagine anyone farming, and under the circumstances, the Papagos have never been able to rely entirely on their crops. The various edible forms of cactus, such seeds and berries as could be found, and the meager hunting of the area rounded out their diet. Even so, the Spanish explorers found them working during part of the year for their richer cousins on the river, as they now work for the big cotton farms outside their desert.

Living in country that is warm for most of the year, the Pimans wore little clothing. They built flat-roofed houses of poles—often digging out the ground inside—walled with cactus rods or brush and some-

Hopi plaques made of coiled basketry. On the middle one is a design representing a Mudhead Kachina

mon among North American Indians. The Pimans' principal religious officials, however, worked their way up through a course of training, and their major ceremonies required priestly control. Once a year, the Papagos fermented a kind of wine from the agave cactus and held a ceremony in which large quantities were drunk to symbolize the soaking of the ground with rain. The result was that everyone went on a pleasant, mild binge, accompanied by music, dancing, prayer, and happy feelings. Ritual intoxication is found in Mexico, but it is rare in North America.

Piman social organization was simple. There were clans, with descent traced through the father, but they ceased to have any function long ago. A village, or group of villages, was governed by a council of elders, presided over by the "Big Man," who was primarily a priest and whose civil authority lay in his reputation for wisdom.

West of the Pimans, on the banks of the Colorado River, were the Yumans—the Yumas and Mohaves—who may be considered as borderline Southwesterners or as Californians who happen to have become involved in farming. Unlike the Pimans, they seem to have farmed because they couldn't help it. Their territory included narrow, extremely fertile areas of flatland along the river that were flooded at regular intervals. Without requiring irrigation, or even much effort, crops grew on these flatlands. So the Yumans planted—or rather their women did, which sets them apart from most of the other Southwesterners. Other differences were that their ceremonies were little concerned with agriculture, and they had no important rites for success in hunting.

The Yumans' farming land was owned by clans or families which traced descent through the father. It was jealously guarded and trespass meant a fight. Men often went naked, the women nearly so, and both sexes were elaborately tattooed. Their houses were like those of the Pimans, but usually larger. Their pottery was fairly good, their basketry simple, their arts in general not highly developed.

Visions or dreams were of great importance to the Yumans and were their prime source of power. It was almost impossible to undertake anything, from fighting to oratory, without having had an appropriate vision. Each tribe or district had a civil leader, whose post was often hereditary but whose authority was purely advisory. However, Brave Man, who led in war, and the Scalp Keeper were of equal importance, and both of these officials received their power from dreams. Scalp-taking was important, and the people danced each month to honor the collection.

times plastered with the clay called "adobe," which becomes extremely hard when it dries. The Papagos, because of the barren nature of their country, could live only in small, widely scattered villages. They were able to come together from time to time for their most important ceremonies. The Pimas were able to live in larger concentrations since, where they lived, it took so much less area to feed a family.

The Pimans made fine basketry and pottery of good quality. In their pottery we encounter a strong Mexican tradition that runs throughout the Southwest. The surface was carefully polished and over it was applied a very fine liquid clay on which, when it dried, designs could be painted.

The Pimans, in their religion, laid great stress on visions and the power that came from visions. This is in keeping with the shamanistic pattern, so com-

The flute, the elaborate face and body paint, and the carefully dressed hair indicate that this young Yuman was all set to go courting. No one knows why he has placed three playing cards by his left foot

Beaded shoulder cloak of a type made both by the Yumas and by the Mohaves

Although made early in this century, these Yuma dolls look much like the work of the ancient Hohokam people

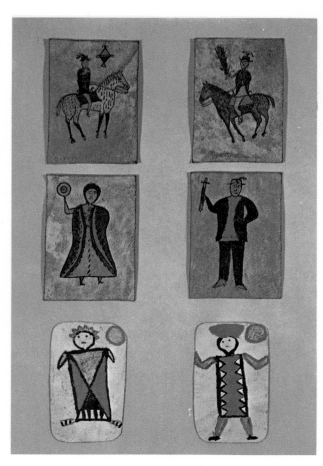

Yuman and (lower) Apache painted buckskin playing cards. The designs on them derive from the Spanish

93

Part of the pueblo at Taos in New Mexico. The ruin of the old church is in the foreground

The interest of the Yumas and Mohaves centered on war, which they seem thoroughly to have enjoyed. They preferred fighting with people of their own general group, who played the game the way they did. In such cases the fighting was formal, with the warriors of both sides drawn up in formation, ceremonious challenges, and duels between men of importance before the fight was opened to the public. Captives were often taken and were brought home, purified, and then either killed or kept as slaves.

Death took on great importance. The Yumans cremated their dead—an unusual custom in North America—on enormous piles of logs laid up with great care. Through the night, while the pyre burned, the dead one's clan danced. Afterwards, the deceased's house was usually burned. Once a year,

relatives of those who had died within the last few years assembled for a feast and ritual lasting for four days. During this ceremony there were many songs and speeches and, at the end, a sham battle.

The Yumans used a weapon in which they took great pride, and with which they were extremely skillful. This was a short club shaped almost exactly like a potato masher except that the handle ended in a spike. You could bash a man's head in with the thick end, or stab him with the spike. The instrument allowed a close in-fighting that would have made even an aggressive Southeasterner think twice.

In yet another way the Southwest differed from the Southeast. In the Southeast, the most nearly civilized tribes were those closest to Mexico; in the Southwest it was those farthest from it—the Pueblos.

94

The modern Pueblo Indians of northern Arizona and New Mexico are in large part descended from the ancient Pueblo Indians who settled in the Southwest 2,000 years ago. Some may be descended from members of other groups—such as the Hohokam—who had moved north. Some are probably descendants of simpler people settled along the Rio Grande, who adopted Pueblo ways when those people moved there from older establishments to the north and west. The main line of culture and racial type is, however, continuous from the ancient Pueblos to those today.

The Pueblos lived in compact towns. In the west, the houses were built of stone cemented with adobe clay. In the east, most houses were built entirely of adobe. Before the arrival of the Spanish, the people did not know how to make square bricks by pouring the mud into forms, so they patted the adobe into "turtlebacks," lumps shaped distinctly like a turtle, and laid them up with a lavish plastering of the same material between layers. Roofs were flat, with a covering of adobe over the top for insulation and to keep out rain. Even so, under heavy rain or if snow was allowed to pile up and melt, these roofs leaked.

Houses were often several stories high, and for defensive purposes were sometimes built without any doors on the ground floor. Ladders, which could be pulled up in time of trouble, led to the upper levels. In each village, usually in a central open space, were the kivas, the ceremonial chambers that also served as clubs or gathering places for the men.

The men farmed, hunted, wove, embroidered, and made jewelry of turquoise, shell, and bright stone. The women did a good deal of the building and all the plastering, cooked, and made pottery and basketry. The men ran the government and controlled the ceremonies, but the women had a lot more to say about these matters than appeared on the surface. A man has to live with his wife, and while it is he who has the say in government, it can become uncomfortable for him at home if he says the wrong thing.

The western Pueblos traced descent through the women, with a strong clan system, strongest of all among the Hopis. Everything went by clans, or by certain lineages within the clans. The fields were clan property, subdivided into family property belonging to the female head of the house. Rituals, ceremonial properties such as masks, priesthoods, and the chieftainships of villages went by clans.

Among the Hopis, "priest" and "chief" are almost interchangeable terms. The Hopi word is *mongwi*, which is usually translated "chief." Every *mongwi*, however, even the Town Chief, is primarily a re-

Inside the kiva. The serpents coming through the screen are manipulated from behind

Zia (upper) and two Acoma pottery jars. Shown on the Zia jar is a roadrunner, a kind of bird often used as decoration by Zia potters

Maria Martinez of San Ildefonso, one of the most famous modern Indian potters

Modern black-on-black jar from San Ildefonso, a style originated by Maria Martinez

Large Cochiti bowl probably made about 1900

Ida Redbird, a Maricopa, polishing bowls

Modern polychrome bowl from San Ildefonso

The designs on the three Pueblo bowls above carry on traditional patterns that started in the late prehistoric period. The lower two bowls are Zuñi, the upper one Hopi

Maria Martinez polishing a bowl before firing it, to give it its high gloss

ligious official. A given chieftainship belongs to the main lineage of a particular clan. The head of the clan is the "clan mother." The old lady has no formal authority, but when she speaks, everyone listens. Someone descended from her will inherit that particular chieftainship, and with it the ceremonial properties that belong to it. The man will marry a woman of another clan, to which his children will belong. A nephew or great-nephew will succeed him.

The father is a guest in his mother-in-law's house. He tends to his sons' education, plays with them, helps them along, but as they are not members of his clan, he will not discipline them. It is the chief member of their clan, their mother's brother, who will discipline them.

Taking over silverworking from the Spanish, the Navahos became the foremost craftsmen in this field in the Southwest. Some examples of their work are shown above and below. The crescent design on the middle necklace, below, came from the Spanish who learned it from the Moors of North Africa. To the Moors, it was a protection from the evil eye

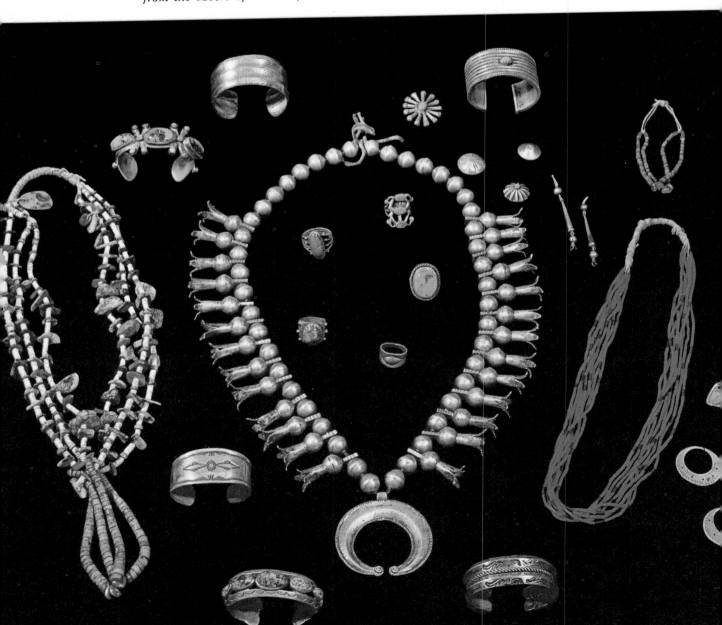

Ornaments and jewelry of the Pueblos. Making ornaments of shell and turquoise is an ancient Pueblo craft. The fine necklace at far left on the page opposite may be of Pueblo manufacture

The Hopis and all other Pueblos have always been monogamous, in contrast to the majority of Indian tribes. Most tribes permitted two or more wives, although many Indians took only one. The monogamy of the Hopis was rather like that of modern American society: a man might marry only one woman at a time, but divorce and remarriage were not difficult.

Eastward from the Hopis, clans become weaker and the mother-descent fades, until along the Rio Grande, among the Tanoans, clans are feeble or non-existent, inheritance is passed through the father, houses and land belong to the men.

With the exception of the village of Moenkopi, founded about a century ago, none of the Hopi villages has water for irrigation. In fact, they are placed in the next most discouraging country for farming after that of the Papagos. Yet by farming the Hopis have lived in that country for a thousand years. They are the supreme dry farmers of the world, and probably the hardest working. Their corn is

scrubby and tough—the stalks hardly three feet high —but it yields fine, big ears. The Hopis have almost given up raising cotton now, since commercial cotton is so easy to come by, but their beans, squash, and tobacco thrive, and to their traditional crops they have added such others as peaches and peanuts.

Along the Rio Grande, where irrigation is possible, conditions have always been much easier. The Pueblos there, especially the northern ones, were in

Blankets, "concho" belts, and hat bands made by the Navahos. These belts are a Navaho specialty

Cornfields at Moencopi in northeastern Arizona. About a century ago, desert-dwelling Hopis settled this village due to its water supply; it is still the only irrigated Hopi settlement

contact with the Plains tribes to the east, which meant both trade and trouble. They had less inhibitions against warfare than most of their Southwestern neighbors, although their fighting was essentially defensive, and their war organizations were elaborate. As their country was too cold for cotton, they did little weaving. Instead they got their cotton garments, kilts for the men, robes for the women, from their relatives to the westward. They also wore more buckskin than the westerners. Most Pueblo

Where there is water for irrigation, as in this San Ildefonso cornfield, modern Pueblo corn grows high

men wore their hair done up in a queue, to be let down during ceremonials. The long, hanging mass represented rain. The northern Pueblos, however, generally adopted the two braids usually associated with the Plains Indians.

All the Pueblos possessed elaborate, formal ceremonies based upon a great body of sacred myths. They perform these ceremonies today virtually as they did centuries ago. Most of the dances, which are dramatized prayers, are strictly disciplined. Every step, every gesture, is exactly rehearsed. There is little room for the individual star; what counts is the perfect performance in union by all concerned. The music, provided by voices accompanied by drums, is composed to fit the sequences of the particular dance. The quality of the performance is not at all wild, and is much more than merely picturesque.

The Wild Animal Hunt Dance, painted by the modern Zia Pueblo artist Ma Pe Wi

The traditional dances of the Pueblos are still performed, and also serve as subject matter for modern Indian artists. Above is the Hopi Tashaf Kachina Dance, painted by Fred Kabotie, one of the most famous modern Indian artists. Below is the Turtle Dance, painted by Pablita Velarde of Santa Clara Pueblo. The figures wearing stripes are koshare, or sacred clowns. The photograph at right is the Buffalo Dance at San Ildefonso

The Sun Dance at San Juan Pueblo

At upper left, a moment in the Hopi Snake Ceremony, one of the rare photographs of 1910. Below it is the Corn Dance, taken in the summer of 1959 at San Ildefonso. At right is the Cochiti Gourd Dance, a painting by the contemporary artist Tonita Peña

Kachina dolls representing the supernatural beings of the Pueblo people. At far left are two Hopi versions of the Zuñi Hemis Kachina; next to them are a Mudhead, a sort of sacred clown, and below it, a Little Fire God. The two dolls above represent the Mountain Goat Kachina

Hopi Kachina dolls

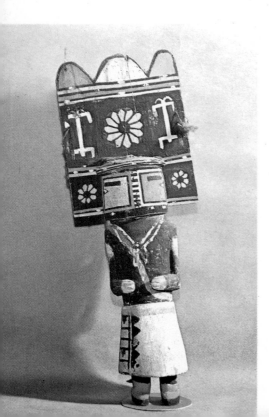

Artists and connoisseurs from many countries throng to see certain of the major public ones.

With the probable exception of those at Taos, in northern New Mexico, all the Pueblos followed what is called the "kachina cult." The kachinas are not gods; they are divine beings who act as intermediates between man and god. Invisible, loving, beneficent, they are present among the people during half the year. In that period—according to instructions they themselves gave to mankind in ancient times—they may be made visible if men who have been properly trained and initiated put on the masks that represent them and dance with the required, exact ritual. Then indeed the kachinas are present. It is not that the masked dancers *are* kachinas, or are thought to be, but that the invisible, real kachinas are there with them.

Unlike the masks of the Iroquois, in the kachina masks there is no attempt to depict human faces, however grotesque. The masks are covered with symbols that express the powers of the kachinas or the good things for which, through them, the people pray—rain, crops, sunlight, fertility.

About nine hundred years ago, the wandering bands speaking Athabascan languages came from the far north into the Southwest. They seem to have

Sand paintings are in reality altars on which the Navahos depict sacred subjects in highly stylized form. They are made quite swiftly, but with great ceremony and ritual

drifted south through great stretches of unoccupied or thinly occupied territory, some of them picking up a few ideas from the primitive tribes of the Great Basin, others from the Western Farmers, until they landed in the Southwest. The Spanish called these people "Apaches." One tribe of this group, called the "Apaches de Nabajú," lived in close contact with the Pueblos. (The Spanish *j* is pronounced *h*.) Later the "Apache" part of the name was dropped and the people became known as the Navahos, one of the most famous of all tribes today.

The various tribes that developed from these wandering bands took over varying aspects of the Southwestern farmers' culture, and also caused the farmers endless trouble. The Navahos learned farming thoroughly. They copied Pueblo rituals, but always with modifications of their own, and merged their northern myths with the rich Pueblo mythology to produce a body of poetic, sacred tales of extraordinary quality.

In the taking of elements from other cultures, the Navahos showed one of their strongest characteristics. Whatever they took, whether from the farming Indians or from the Spanish, they took only in the form that suited their way of life. The Pueblos lived in compact groups in which everyone knew everyone else's business, and in which each individual was kept in line by the force of unremitting public opinion. Each group was tightly organized, every individual exactly placed, all under the government of the priestly chiefs.

The Navahos wanted no such life. They liked individuality and elbow room, and placed their dwellings accordingly. They took over a great deal of Pueblo ritual, but fitted it always to their own basic religion. Their primary concern was to keep themselves in harmony with God and all His creation. The clearest symptom of being out of harmony was illness, hence their ceremonies centered upon healing a patient, while at the same time being intended to ensure benefits for all. The Pueblos painted sacred, stylized pictures with dry pigments on the floors of their kivas for certain rites. The Navahos took over this idea, elaborated it enormously into their famous "sand paintings," consisting of hundreds of symbolic pictures that are reproduced with great care from memory according to the ceremony being performed, and tied it into their healing-harmony pattern.

Only the right hand is used to apply the pigments

The sand painting is begun with its central motif

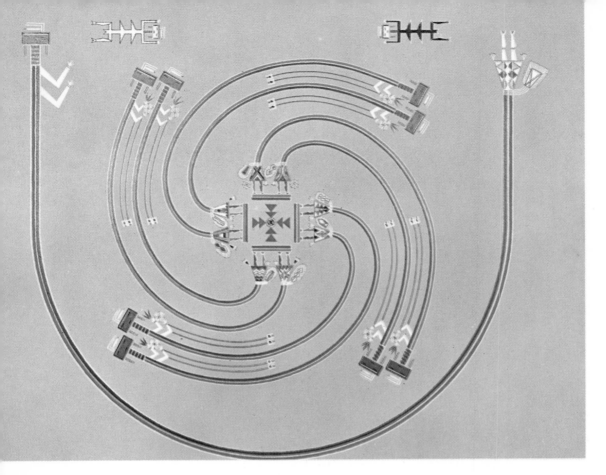

Swirling Rainbow Goddesses

Painting on Roof of Sweat House

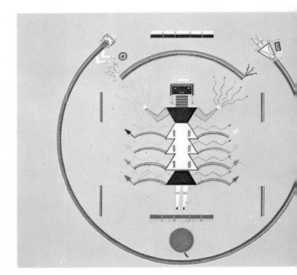

Big Wind Chant

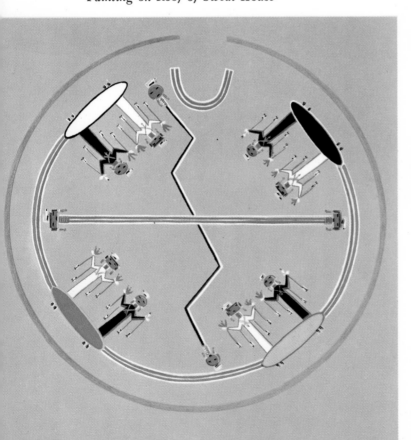

Sand paintings are made for chants or ceremonies. At upper left is one used in a rite held in summer to bring rain and ensure good crops. In its center is a series of Rainbow Girls or Goddesses, and it is enclosed by another Rainbow Girl for protection

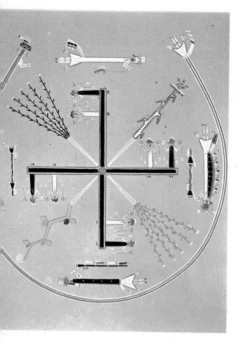

Whirling Logs from Night Chant

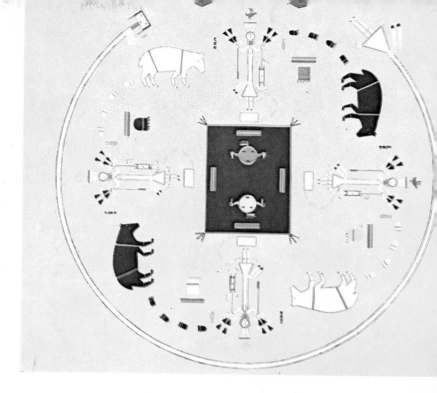

Four Bears from Mountain Chant

Sunflower Gods

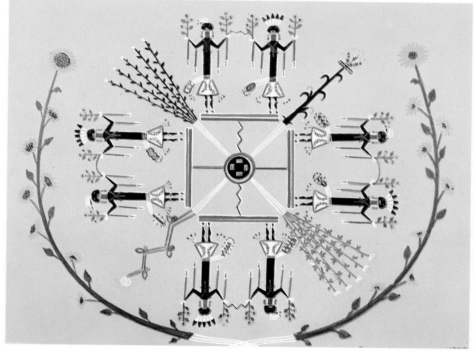

Water Creatures from Beauty Chant

Sand paintings are different for each ceremony or chant. Ceremonies that last more than a day—and some last nine days and nights—have a different sand painting for each day. At the conclusion of each day's ceremony, the sand painting that was made for that day is destroyed

107

A characteristic Navaho scene—a woman weaves, another tends a baby, a small boy studies the loom. Children find looms irresistible, which is a considerable trial for their mothers

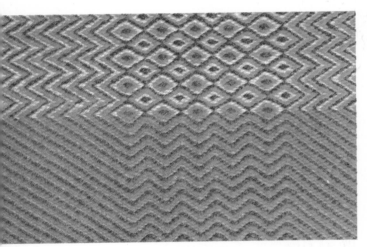

An example of Navaho craftsmanship in weaving: four different patterns have been skillfully woven into a single rug. Such work is the more astonishing as it is all done on hand looms, like the one shown above

The Navahos became great farmers and later great herders. They could have lived comfortably in peace. But they continued to be warriors and raiders, adding what they could take by stealth or by force to the products of their own industry.

They learned weaving from the Pueblos, probably from captives whom they enslaved, but left it to their women to do. After the Spanish introduced wool, the Navahos became the outstanding weavers of North America. Their designs, however, are totally unlike those of the Pueblos. Much later, they learned silversmithing from the Spanish, and became the finest silverworkers of the Southwest.

The Navahos also copied the strong mother clans of the western Pueblos, but without such elements as the clan mother. A man became a permanent guest in his wife's home—unless she decided to divorce him.

A common sight on the reservation—blankets hanging in the sun before a neat, modern, eight-sided hogan

Among the Pueblos, the home was openly dominated by the old mother. Among the Navahos, the new couple built a separate dwelling and it was forbidden for a man and his mother-in-law to see or speak to each other.

The traditional Navaho dwelling is the *hogan* (pronounced hoe-GAHN). Its original form was a framework of heavy poles set up like a tepee, with a small vestibule at the entrance—suggesting a cross between a tepee and an earth lodge. It had a tepee-like smoke hole and was covered with a heavy layer of earth. Later, this was elaborated into an eight-sided building with a domed roof. In recent times, walls have been made of stone. It would not, however, occur to the Navahos to save effort by building a series of rooms in a single unit in which many families could live in close contact.

Above, a hogan in winter. Below, Navaho rugs, the earliest of which (the two in the upper left corner) were woven in the 1850's, the latest (in the center) in 1950

Mario Martinez, a Navaho chief, sketched about 1850. Except for the cloth strip around his head and the braid down his back, he is dressed in the Spanish style

Wife of the head of Jemez Pueblo and (below) a Navaho

Navaho woman and child, photographed at the time of the Bosque Redondo captivity. The expression on her face sums up the tribe's feeling about this experience

Originally the Navahos must have dressed, much like other Apaches, in buckskin with simple or no ornamentation, and worn their hair hanging loose over their shoulders. Upon contact with the Pueblos, they took over such articles of Pueblo woven clothing as the short, poncholike shirt. The women partly copied the blue and black woven robe of the Pueblo women. However, the Pueblo form is a single piece worn over one shoulder and under the other; the Navaho form is in two pieces, usually joined over both shoulders. With their usual exuberance, the Navaho women wove strips of brilliant red into their dresses. This women's costume was replaced during the last half of the nineteenth century by the velveteen blouses and very full, swinging calico skirts

Chapatan, chief of the San Juan Navahos. Unlike Martinez, he is wearing clothes that seem to be in the traditional Navaho style showing no influence from Spain

Young Navaho warrior at Bosque Redondo. The crude leggings that reach from his moccasins almost to his knees are buckskin; his quiver is made out of lion skin

The favorite wife of Manuelito, principal chief of the Navahos, photographed in Washington in 1874 while on a journey there with her husband. She is wearing a most handsome silver "concho" belt. Below is the governor of the Jemez Pueblo, sketched in the mid-19th century. His wife is shown in the upper corner of the page opposite

that are worn by Navaho women to this day. Both sexes took to doing their hair at the back in the Pueblo-style queue.

Navaho culture is so curious a blend that it would take a book to analyze it—if we were able to sort out all the items. There are elements from the original, northern Athabascan culture, from the early Plains and the Pueblos, and other elements from the tribes of the Great Basin behind the Rockies. Thus, the Navahos occasionally made pottery that is distinctly eastern, while their baskets are difficult to tell from those of the wandering tribes of southern Utah. Their "medicine men" are lone operators, like shamans, but in fact they are priests, trained in certain myths and ceremonies, after the Pueblo model.

The Yeibichai Dance in front of a hogan, by the modern Navaho artist Harrison Begay

The goal of Navaho religion was to create beauty and happiness in man and nature by achieving harmony between man, nature, and God. Their creative gift and imagination enabled the Navahos to elaborate their weaving, silversmithing, and sandpainting to a considerable degree. This creativity was also responsible for the development of a remarkable range of ceremonies, some lasting nine days and nights, and a body of myths and prayers of high poetic quality.

Navaho mask of the Child of the Water, the younger of the twin war gods and taker of the first scalp. The symbols that resemble hourglasses represent scalps

Fringe mouth mask, representing one of a family of supernatural beings

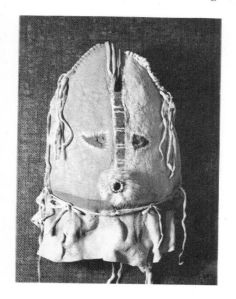

Harrison Begay's "Feather Dance." The feathered disks held by the dancers are connected by strings to the single central disk. Since the dance takes place at night, the audience is unable to see the strings and the central disk seems to move up and down by itself

The Yeibichai, or Grandfather of the Gods, dominates the dance named after him. In this painting by Harrison Begay, the Yeibichai is the figure at the upper left

113

19th century Apache necklace and beadwork

Buckskin shirt of the San Carlos Apaches

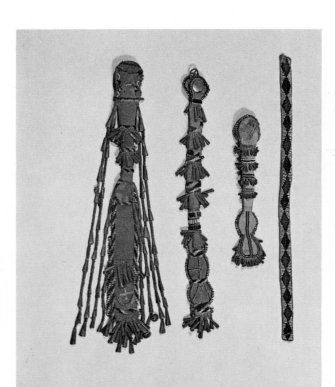

Along the eastern border of New Mexico, the Apache tribes—the Jicarilla Apaches in the north, the Mescaleros in the south, and the now all-but-extinct Lipans roaming through western Texas and into Mexico—were a bridge between the culture of the Plains and that of the Southwest. The Jicarillas look like most Plains Indians, with their tepees, their braided hair, and their buckskin clothing handsomely adorned with fine beadwork. Many of their customs reflect those of the Plains, but in early times they raised corn, beans, and squash, and their principal ceremony combines sand paintings, a Navaho-Pueblo-type masked dance, a Basin-type dance of men and women together, and the old Athabascan pattern of the ceremony performed at night, by bonfires, within an enclosure of green branches.

The Mescaleros showed little Pueblo influence and had little interest in farming. Based in mountains where the hunting was good, with access to buffalo country, they were hunters and raiders. They used both the tepee and the "wickeyup," a dwelling made of branches and grass laid over a framework of poles, either with a rounded roof, or a pointed one. At their best, these wickeyups sometimes resembled the Wichita grass houses, sometimes suggested wigwams, and sometimes were clearly tepees with a different covering.

The wickeyup was the typical home of the other Apaches, the tribes that sifted down through the Pueblo country into the heart of the Southwest and on into northern Mexico. When there was peace, and the people were able to stay in one place for a

Apache wickeyup, or brush shelter, at "Indian City," Anadarko, Oklahoma, and (left) awl cases and headband

reasonable time, they built elaborate, large, comfortable residences. In time of war they built simple shelters, hastily thrown together. An Apache band could break camp and be gone in a matter of minutes.

The Apache bands roamed about, gathering a great variety of edible seeds and wild plants, hunting, and watching for chances for a raid. Government was democratic. There were families from which chiefs were expected to come, but if a man of no special family had sufficient ability, others began following him, and soon he was in fact a chief. The shifting organization and the movement of the people themselves make it difficult to arrive at a satisfactory listing of western Apache tribes. A "tribe" was a number of Apaches speaking one dialect, having the same customs and religious practices, and recognizing a certain likeness, rather than unity, among themselves. Tribes gathered under strong leaders.

To the Apaches and Navahos, war was a business. Properly speaking, it was not war, but armed robbery accompanied by acts of brutality. The purpose was to obtain booty and, occasionally, slaves. Obviously it was a dangerous occupation, but it was foolish to run needless risks. The object was to get the booty and come home without loss, if such could be managed. For this the young men were rigorously trained in boyhood. They had to undergo such toughening exercises as running several miles in the hottest weather with a mouthful of water, spitting out the water at the end to show they had not swallowed it, and such combat training as standing and dodging arrows shot at them by others.

Chiricahua Apache Mountain Spirit Dancer, by Momaday

Large basket jar made about 1920 by San Carlos Apaches

The Apaches were expert basket makers; they may have learned the art from the Basin people

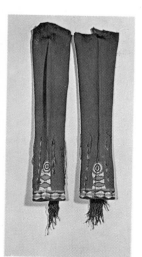

Mescalero Apache buckskin leggings

Examples of Southwestern basketry

Chiricahua Apache headdress decorated with fur, hair, and the horns of an antelope

Jicarilla Apache shield with quiver and bow, and arrows of the old type with stone heads

Geronimo, his son, and two of his followers photographed in 1886, shortly before he surrendered to General Crook

They became as hardy as human beings can be, skilled in combat, incredibly observant, and gifted at concealment to a degree that seems like magic. All of these qualities stood them in good stead after the white men came and pressed upon them. Cochise, for instance, with less than two hundred warriors, held the U. S. Army at bay for over ten years and forced the government in the end to make peace with an unconquered enemy.

The Spanish settlement of the Southwest in the 1590's was almost entirely in the Pueblo area along the Rio Grande. Missionaries and small military expeditions reached eastwards to the Hopis. Unlike the English, the Spanish were not land-hungry colonizers; they came in relatively small numbers to conquer, Christianize, and exploit the natives. They did not, therefore, seek to drive the Pueblos off their land, but wanted to keep them on it as a source of labor and taxes. The free-moving Athabascans eluded the Spanish grasp, and it was not until later that the priests reached the Pimans.

The Spanish hand lay heavy. The old religion was forbidden, forced labor was close to slavery, taxes drew off the corn and the woven goods, and there were churches and priests to support. Ninety years after the first Spanish town was founded, the Pueblos achieved what none of the eastern tribes had been able to manage—perfect concerted action. Under the leadership of a man named Popé, from the pueblo of San Juan, on one day they all arose—from the villages on the Rio Grande to the Hopis 250 miles and more westward. Mission priests were killed, and the Indians fell upon outlying ranches. The Navahos and some other Apaches gladly joined in.

Santa Fe was besieged, and in a short time the Spanish were forced to abandon it. Their retreat did not end until they reached El Paso, "The Ford," the crossing of the Rio Grande into Mexico. That was in 1680. It was not until 1693 that they were able to march back into Santa Fe.

Until the Pueblo Rebellion, the Spanish had kept close watch on their horses. Indians had been for-

116

Apache shelter in wartime—Geronimo's camp at the time of his capture

Wearing an old fighting costume, a modern White Mountain Apache poses on horseback for his picture

Measuring cloth to be issued to the Indians at San Carlos, 1887. At right is a sergeant of the Apache scouts of the U.S. Cavalry

bidden to own the animals, and the herds were guarded. During the twelve-odd years of Indian independence the animals ran wild and multiplied, and the Navahos and Apaches discovered their usefulness. After the Spanish returned, their horses were constantly stolen. Thus one of the white men's most important weapons passed into Indian hands.

The Pueblos along the Rio Grande submitted again to Spain. They became Christian, but also kept up their old religion, more and more boldly as Spanish military power in this far corner of a dying empire grew weaker. Since ceremonies were forbidden, the Indians made them secret, and even today no white man may see a Pueblo masked dance.

In the western section, the Spanish and their priests were never able to reestablish themselves among the Zuñis and Hopis. These tribes, therefore, never adopted the "double-barreled" religion of the more easterly people, in whose villages church and kiva stand in sight of each other. Nor did they make their ceremonies secret, and a well-behaved visitor

may witness among them today the sacred rites that have come down through centuries.

The Spanish may have caused the Pueblos a lot of grief, but they also brought iron and steel tools, wagons, draft animals, wheat, fruit trees, sheep, and cattle, all of which made farming much more productive. They taught the Indians the ancient Mediterranean-Asian art of making adobe bricks in molds, which enabled them to build larger houses.

Meantime the Navahos and Apaches were growing bolder, and to the eastward appeared tribes of whom no one had ever heard before: the Kiowas and Comanches, mounted raiders from the Plains. From the early 1700's to the American annexation of the Southwest in 1846, the Pueblos and the Spanish stood back to back, fighting off the wild tribes that endlessly harried them.

Warfare in the Southwest, as elsewhere among North American Indians, seldom aimed at the total destruction of the enemy. Just as earlier the Pueblos had alternated between fighting and trading with

117

the Athabascans, so they repeated the pattern with the mounted Comanches. The horsemen wanted corn; the Pueblos wanted buffalo meat and hides. The trading center was at Taos. The Spanish encouraged this trade with their enemies, because they wanted slaves, which, in response to their demand, the Comanches provided in the form of captives from other tribes.

In historic times the Navahos and Apaches also took slaves. Children and women usually wound up as members of the tribe. Among the Navahos today, there are a number of clans that trace their origin to women captured from various alien tribes.

The Spanish came in small numbers; so at first did the settlers from the east whose descendants are known in the Southwest as "Anglo-Americans." Much of the land the Indians occupied was unattractive to white men (unless there were known to be minerals in it); some of it was downright repulsive. As a result, most of the Southwestern tribes got large reservations of their own land, and were allowed to keep them. By the time the pressure to obtain Indian land became strong, the national conscience had changed and the old custom of tearing up the treaties could no longer be followed.

There were breaches of faith, of course. Many of the Pueblos lost chunks of their land, for which they were later compensated. The Chiricahuas, after being at peace for a generation, were forcibly uprooted from the reservation they had honorably won for themselves under Cochise. There were other, similar instances, but the Indians of the Southwest today hold the largest unbroken tracts of land remaining to any tribes. In addition, fewer of the tribes have become extinct, most make a tolerable living, and they have been able also to retain more of their cultures than can be found anywhere else in the United States.

Of all the Southwestern tribes, the Navahos have had the strangest history. In 1868, the great frontiersman Kit Carson finally gave them the trouncing they so richly deserved. The greater part of the tribe, about eight thousand in all, surrendered and went on "the long walk" from their homeland along the Arizona-New Mexico border to Bosque Redondo in eastern New Mexico. There wild theorists thought that many people could become happy and prosperous on forty square miles of inferior land with insufficient water. The crops they planted failed. They went hungry. The Comanches raided them. After four years, by which time their condition had become a public scandal and even the hardboiled newspapers of New Mexico were supporting them, they were returned to a reservation in their own country, issued two head of sheep apiece, and given tools. There they were joined by an estimated four thousand more who had never been rounded up.

One thing was certain—their experience had converted them to peace. They fell to work to restore themselves as farmers, herdsmen, and craftsmen. Their flocks increased rapidly, and so did they. The land in which they lived was so rugged, much of it so arid, and so remote, that no one wanted it. Their reservation was enlarged many times, to about the size of West Virginia. On some of this vast area today it takes forty acres to maintain one cow for a year. On parts of it nothing can be raised; it is pure rock.

Most of the Navahos were hostile to the white men's culture and therefore to schooling. The reservation was enormous and almost without roads. No one knew how many Navahos there were; estimates in the late 1920's ran around twenty-five thousand. Few schools were built; only a fraction of the tribe even learned to speak English. Still they increased,

and still, egged on by all the officials who dealt with them, they increased their flocks. The number of their sheep and horses far exceeded what the arid land could support, and the land began to deteriorate rapidly. Where there had been brooks, there developed deep-cut arroyos. With the disappearance of the watercourses the underground water level dropped, taking the fertility from the high ground. With the grass eaten off, the violent thunderstorms washed off the topsoil, which ended in the Colorado River where it is helping shorten the life of Boulder Dam.

In 1933 the government awoke and decreed a drastic reduction of stock, with grazing only according to the number that could be nourished. It had to be done, but it was done clumsily and too hastily, and however it was done, it shattered the Navaho economy and changed the life of the tribe. The Navahos have never recovered from the shock of it. They were eating well; they were independent; they were doing all right—then everything was turned upside down.

When ration books were issued in World War II, we began to discover how many Navahos there were —over sixty thousand of them! In 1960 the best estimate is eighty-five thousand—a great body of people increasing rapidly, on a tract of land that can support, at best, twenty-five thousand. Few have been to school, pathetically few have a real command of English. Poverty is intense and agonizing.

The Navahos took a long look at their own problem and decided that what they needed above everything was education—a school seat for every child, no matter if all the adults went hungry. This the government has finally provided, as part of a promising "rehabilitation program" enacted by Congress. What is most impressive is what the Navahos are doing for themselves, through their tribal council under a succession of able chairmen. The council consists of seventy-two delegates, some of whom are well educated, some of whom speak no English. It has become an effective governing body of real vision.

By great good fortune, much of the Navaho country turns out to have oil, uranium, or other minerals in it, so that the tribe in recent years has received as much as five million dollars in one year. Resisting the temptation to pass any of this money around in handouts, the council has appropriated it for purposes of

more efficient government, for an anti-tuberculosis program, for sending young Navahos to college, and for development of industries and enterprises that will bring long-term income and create steady jobs for Navahos. One of the council's acts has been to appropriate three hundred thousand dollars to assist towns adjacent to the reservation in bringing in industries that will employ Navahos—and this by a people over 60% illiterate, voted by men in business suits and by men with turquoise in their ears and sacred pollen in their medicine pouches. The situation the Navahos face is still grave, but if there is any tribe that will help itself, it is this one.

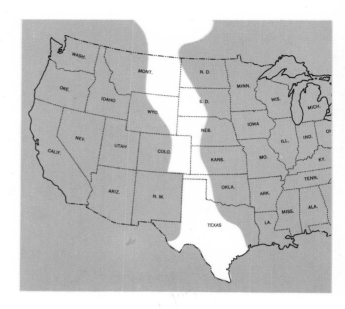

Buffalo hide shield of Bull Elk,
a Crow chief, made around 1860

The Great Open Spaces

"Warrior Sacrificing His Horse" by George Catlin. The
artist lived among the Indians and his paintings of the
Farmers and Plains Indians show us how these people
lived before they were overwhelmed by white settlers

Between the slopes of the Rocky Mountains on
the west and the twenty-inch rainfall line on the
east, from north of the Canadian border down to the
Rio Grande in western Texas, lies the vast area of
the High Plains. It is one of the world's great grazing
areas, the ancient range of millions of buffalo.

The higher cultures of the Southeast and Southwest
reached into the Plains only feebly. Out there you
could plant gardens only in favored spots in river
bottoms, and even so, in a dry year you might not
make a crop. Before there were horses or metal
weapons, people used to a good life based on large-
scale farming would make hunting expeditions for
buffalo meat, but they would not choose to live in
such country. At the time of the earliest French and
Spanish reports, the High Plains were occupied by
humble people of Athabascan speech, bands of
Apaches whom we call Paducahs. They hunted on
foot, and did their best to copy the farming of their
more advanced neighbors to the west and east.

As told in the previous chapter, the Spanish horses
ran wild and spread east and north through the
Plains after the Pueblo Rebellion of 1680. Also,

Crow Indians, from a sketch by Bodmer in 1833. Three of the men wear buffalo robes

horses from the Spanish settlements in California spread up along the West Coast and into Oregon. Various tribes in the Northwest, inland from the sea, captured horses and began raising them. The Cayuse tribe became so outstanding at breeding horses that "cayuse" later became a cowboy word for horse. The Palouse developed a breed of roan horses with white hindquarters and white horses with roan hindquarters that continues to this day, still known as "Palousian" or "Appalousian." They are somewhat taller than most western horses, fast and strong, and excellent for working cattle.

The Indians of the northwestern mountains traded horses to those farther east. Wild horses came up from the south. First the Paducahs became horsemen, and with this advantage harried the Pawnees and other Caddoan tribes, then, about the middle of the eighteenth century, the Uto-Aztecan Comanches from Wyoming swept into the Plains and fell upon the Paducahs. The Algonkian Cheyennes and Arapahos abandoned their farms and moved west, so did the Crows, close relatives of the Mandans. The Algonkian Blackfeet on the Canadian border, and

Extract from a Sioux "winter count" giving events of 1540, the year White Buffalo Woman came to the Sioux and taught them their religion and ceremony

121

An encampment of the Blackfeet in northern Montana about 1850. Entering at left is a group of visiting Crees, coming to trade arms and other goods. The Crees lived in Canada slightly to the east of the Blackfeet. They obtained trading materials from the French and English and passed them on to tribes farther west. The upraised arms of the two leaders means that they are meeting in a spirit of peace. Some of the Blackfeet warriors, like medieval knights, display their shields before their tepees

the Sioux, who had been Woodland Hunters, took up the new life centered upon the buffalo. This life was made possible by horses and by white men's goods—weapons, including firearms, and metal tools —obtained through trade from the east.

The change happened with surprising speed. In the 1760's the more easterly Sioux tribes were still primarily canoe Indians; by 1796 they had abandoned the use of canoes and taken completely to horses. Before then the Kiowas of Montana, whose language is related to the Pueblo Tanoan, acquired horses and

moved into the panhandle country of Oklahoma and Texas. There they became neighbors of the Comanches, with whom they joined in industriously raiding the Spanish and Pueblo settlements.

The Paducahs were unable to stand against these invaders. Most of them retreated into the Southwest, joining their Apache relatives there. One group, now called the Kiowa Apaches, joined the Kiowas, becoming something on the order of poor relations. In southwest Texas, the Lipan Apaches remained in the Plains until the white men conquered them. In

Canada, the Athabascan Sarsi are attached to the Blackfeet; they were not Paducahs, but more closely related to the Athabascans of the north.

Those tribes that had farmed, such as the Cheyennes, forgot about it, or continued only the ceremonial planting of small plots of tobacco. The Western Farmers greatly stepped up their pursuit of the buffalo. For horsemen, hunting the big beasts became an exciting and profitable sport. With horses, too, the hides necessary to make really big tepees could easily be carried, long tepee poles could be

dragged, and the animals could carry the tribe's belongings as the people moved.

When the buffalo were in their territory, the tribes lived richly. There was more than enough to eat. During the time when the buffalo were away, which for most tribes was the winter, the pickings were not so good. The Indians stored as much meat as they could by jerking it—slicing it thin and sun-drying it. They made pemmican by pounding dried meat, mixing it with dried, crushed berries, putting it in sacks, and pouring melted fat and bone marrow over the mixture. It was nutritious; but according to white men who tried it, it was a pretty nasty dish that took some getting used to. Those tribes that controlled mountain country moved into it for the winter deer hunting, the others hunted what they could find on the Plains. Most of them, in the lean months, broke up into small groups, as there was not enough food in one place for the whole tribe.

In due course the buffalo came back. They always came back. It was a mystery; the great animals disappeared, and in season returned in their thousands, predictably, as certain as spring itself. Inevitably, many religious beliefs clustered around them. By spring, the tribe was assembled again waiting for the buffalo—perhaps a thousand or more of the gleaming, tall tents grouped in a great semi-circle. At night, if a bright fire was burning in one of them, the whole tent glowed like a lantern.

Then one day scouts came in with the news that the buffalo were coming. The ordinarily lax discipline of the tribe immediately became strict. The police, selected young warriors, in many tribes the members of the Dog Society, took over to restrain any over-eager hunter who might frighten the great herd away. A hunter who went ahead on his own might be whipped or his tepee and all his belongings might be burned. All had to act together, swooping upon the herd, if possible, in such a way as to get the animals milling about before each man went in for the kill. The men were mounted on their "buffalo horses," fast animals trained to come up alongside a buffalo and stay in just the right position for a lance thrust or a close-in shot with bow or gun.

While the first of the game was being butchered, the liver was sliced and eagerly eaten raw. It was packed with vitamins, and after their winter diet, the people were suffering vitamin starvation. White men who wintered with the Indians, or in the same manner, found themselves craving a delicacy that otherwise would have revolted them.

If the hunt was successful the village was full of food. Everyone feasted. There was leisure for art. They painted their tepees and adorned them with medallions of beadwork. They decorated everything that would take decoration, the men by painting, the women with lavish porcupine-quill embroidery, and shortly thereafter with the rich beadwork that produced some of the handsomest costumes in the world. And while the women were busy tanning and working hides and drying meat, the men had leisure and plenty of energy for fun and games—and the greatest game of all was war.

124

Camp of the Piegans, a division of the Blackfeet, painted by Bodmer. The Plains Indians gathered in large groups for the summer buffalo-hunting season

Painted buffalo-hide robe of a Cheyenne warrior. Robes such as this were commonly worn by Plains Indians, the men frequently decorating theirs with personal records. Robes were usually made from the entire buffalo hide

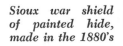

Sioux war shield
of painted hide,
made in the 1880's

Gros Ventre shield
with the body of a
hawk attached to it

The designs and ornaments on shields were revealed
in visions and had great significance to the owner

Mounted Sioux hunters chasing buffalo, a painting by Catlin done in the 1830's. The
practice was for all the hunters to sweep down at once upon a herd, and once it was
in a state of confusion, to go in for the kill. This took courage and well-trained horses

Sioux dress made prior to 1854 and decorated with elks' teeth

Sioux dress, beaded and fringed and made for a child. It is a duplicate of a dress that an adult would wear

Sioux beaded moccasins

Above, a Sioux shirt made sometime in the last quarter of the 19th century; left, decorated Hunkpapa Sioux shirt

Elaborately beaded and decorated baby carrier, typical of the Kiowas

From left to right, Blackfeet, Cheyenne, and Sioux tobacco pouches, made during the 1880's and decorated with glass beads obtained from white men

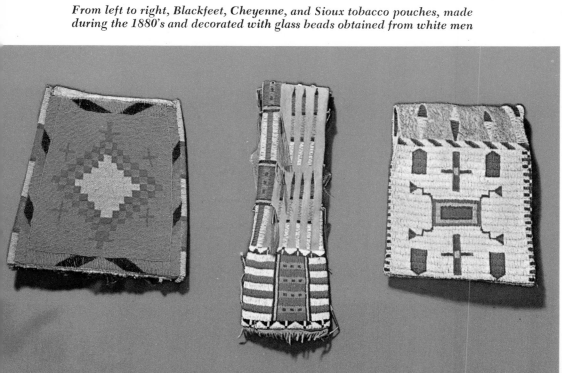

Blackfeet knife sheath decorated with beads

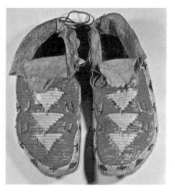

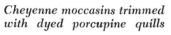
Cheyenne moccasins trimmed with dyed porcupine quills

Artifacts from the buffalo. Crow shield; Sioux pipe bag and parfleche; Crow, Sioux, and Cree moccasins; Sioux buffalo horn spoon; Cree drum; Blackfeet pouch

Model of a decorated Kiowa tepee cover of buffalo skin. One half of it shows a lively battle with United States troops

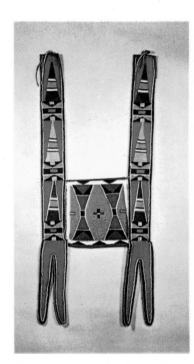
Chest ornament for horse, Crow

Scenes from the life of the painter including, midway down the robe, a self-portrait showing the painter on horseback are shown on this Kiowa robe of about 1900. Indians only rarely painted self-portraits, but robes of this sort, showing an adventure or incident of daily life, are quite common among Indians of the Plains

127

One of several autobiographical drawings by the Sioux leader Sitting Bull. The buffalo (upper right) identifies him. He is counting coup on a Crow whose gun narrowly misses him

Almost every important element in Plains horseback culture came from outside the High Plains area, be it the white men's horses or the war-game pattern derived from the Western Farmers. On the whole, the farming tribes living west of the Mississippi contributed most to what became the colorful Plains pattern. We nowadays think of this kind of war as being above all a game played by the horseback hunters, and it was among those purely hunting tribes that it reached its height.

It was all done in a spirit of fun, with the principal object to gain glory or avenge an attack. The most common practice was for a single man, or a party of men, to sneak up on another tribe's camp and see how many horses they could run off with. It was especially honorable to go right into the village center and steal the favorite horse of some important warrior, which was kept tethered near his tent. Horses were stolen not for economic reasons but for glory—the tribes already had more of the animals than they could use.

As with the tribes to the east, it was more important to run risks than to kill, and although scalps were taken, few tribes gave special honors for them. Some men carried poles adorned with feathers, coup sticks, as their only weapon. Not killing the enemy, but stealing a picketed horse, snatching a bow or gun, or making a coup were important. (Coup, pronounced "coo," is simply the French word for "blow.") A coup could be made by touching the enemy with a bare hand or stick, or killing him with a hand weapon. If someone *shot* an enemy, whether with a gun or bow and arrow, not the shooter but the first man to run up and touch the body got the high honor.

When certain young Sioux came back from France after World War I, they asked the old men to initiate them into the soldier societies. It turned out that, while these young men had killed a fair number of Germans, it had all been done by shooting. None of them had been in a bayonet fight, none had actually touched an enemy. Shooting people with rifles might be a useful thing to do under certain circumstances, but as a qualification for rank among warriors, it did not count. They were refused initiation.

The war game was, of course, deadly. Nobody aimed to get killed, but plenty were killed. To keep the game honest, the tribe that was being raided, if it detected the raiders before they got away, did its level best to kill them. So, too, when two war parties met, the man who rushed in with a coup stick was likely to be met with arrows or lances.

"Sioux Teacher," by Oscar Howe. The man describes to the boys the exploits painted on his tepee. Plains Indians had no modesty about depicting or telling about their achievements, but they had to be absolutely accurate or they would be disgraced

He Who Jumps Over All, a Crow warrior, painted by Catlin. The long hair streaming out behind was typical of Crow warriors, but horses were dressed up in "war bonnets" only on very special occasions

Cheyenne necklace made around 1876. High Wolf, its owner, adorned it with left-hand middle fingers of enemies slain in battle

Sioux roach and (below) Mandan bonnet with ermine tails and eagle feathers. Below at left is a Blackfeet medicine society bonnet decorated with ermine tails and buffalo horns

True warfare also occurred, usually because one tribe wanted to move into another tribe's territory. This happened when the Paducahs were driven out. The Shoshones, known to early explorers as Snakes, came into the Plains with the Comanches; the Sioux drove them back. They and many other tribes in the Rocky Mountains and to the north and east wanted to get into the act—tribes such as the Utes, the Jicarilla Apaches, the Nez Percés, the Crees in Canada and the more westerly of the Chippewas, who had originally driven the Sioux out of the woodlands and now provided them with fine fighting. All of these tribes adopted more or less of Plains ways, so that the line where the Plains culture ends cannot easily be drawn. It blends into the culture of the surrounding areas.

War achievement led to honors and rank. Many of the men whom whites called "chiefs" were simply warriors who had proved their mettle, were honored accordingly, and were chosen to lead war parties. They had no governmental authority. The list of honorable deeds varied from tribe to tribe. Generally it included leading a successful war party, one that stole horses or killed enemies or made coups, and on which no one from the home tribe was killed.

Two Sioux leaders, War Eagle of the Yankton Sioux (left) and Red Cloud of the Oglala Sioux, in the 1880's. Red Cloud's single feather was more usual than the full regalia worn by War Eagle

A Sioux chief's funeral scaffold in 1834. Placing the dead on scaffolds rather than burying them may have originated in Asia. The bones were later placed in rock crevices

A successful Crow captain of war parties trimmed his shirt and moccasins with hair; one who had struck coups attached wolf tails to the heels of his moccasins; the warrior who had snatched a gun or bow decorated his shirt with ermine skins. The Blackfeet also used decorations of ermine skins to indicate honors. Many tribes, the Sioux more than any others, developed a "feather heraldry," by which eagle feathers worn in the hair or in a headdress told of the wearer's achievements. From this developed the familiar "war bonnet," with or without the tail of feathers hanging down the back. In early illustrations, we see the tail fairly often, attached to a headdress of skin with a pair of horns attached to it. Entirely feathered war bonnets are less common.

As we might expect when people move into a territory from many different directions—in this case from the east, north, and west—they differed in many ways. For example, in the Plains and the areas immediately surrounding them were six different language families and more than twenty-two separate languages. As a means of communication, the tribes developed a "sign language," a system of gestures by which intricate conversations could be carried on.

"And They Moved Without Him," by the modern artist Black Bear Bosin. The heads and tails of the dead man's favorite horses are tied onto the scaffold

Winter games of the Cheyenne. Women gambling, a "stick-in-the-hoop" game, tops, wrestling, dancing, sledding, and a "snow-snake" javelin game are included among the festivities

As usual in North America, war and peace alternated, often in rapid succession. The tribes were wide-ranging; friendly as well as hostile dealings might occur between any of them. During time of peace there was trade—not only of goods but of ideas. Eventually, all the tribes adopted a similar material culture in that such things as their clothing, tents, tools, and diet became very much alike.

Material culture is the easiest thing to imitate. An Indian who saw a large, handsomely painted tepee made one like it, if he had the necessary skins and poles, and painted it. But unless he had spent some time talking to the owner of the first tent, he did not know what symbolic or sacred meanings the decorations may have had; instead he used meanings and designs of his own. Non-material culture spreads more slowly. The war-and-honor pattern is an example of non-material culture, consisting mainly of a number of ideas that reached to almost all the tribes.

Some of these tribes had clans that traced descent through the mother, others, clans that traced it through the father, some had no clans. Among some, a husband moved to his wife's camp; among others, the other way round. Most of them had a somewhat romantic pattern of courtship, including playing tunes on simple flutes. Elopements occurred, but the preferred custom was courtship followed by the formal purchase of the bride from her family. The purchase price was paid in horses. This does not mean that the bride was "sold." The number of horses paid for her was a testimony both to the husband's love for her and the high esteem in which her family held her.

Tribal organization was loose and democratic. At special times, as during a hunt, the police imposed rigid discipline; at other times public opinion was the main force. Chiefs were respected; they were advisers but they did not give orders. If two men started a fight, chiefs might come between them carrying sacred pipes and urge them to stop, but no force was used. Among the Cheyennes, who had a complex system of law, murder was taken very gravely. It damaged the whole tribe. It profaned the Sacred Arrows, their holiest possession and the center of their sacred power. The murderer came before the council of chiefs, and faced an exile of as long as ten years.

Among the Crow, murder was a private matter between the killer's clan and the victim's. The police came into the picture, not to make an arrest or to punish, but to try to persuade the killer and his people to make an adequate payment to the bereaved, to avoid the starting of a harmful feud.

The power of public opinion was great. The Blackfeet had a system of mockery that could make life intolerable to a man and drive him out alone on a quest for death or war honors with which to redeem himself. In some tribes, it was a particular relative's duty to rebuke a man who had behaved badly. The rebuke was given publicly, and the shame of it was an intense punishment.

Children's playthings made probably by the Sioux in the late 19th century. These toys include a small seated buffalo, a male doll, and a colorful American elk, or wapiti

Sioux women playing ball, painted by George Catlin. In this fast and lively game, a small hair ball was struck with a curved stick made of cherry wood. It was a favorite summer sport of Plains women. Judging by the picture, any number could play

Pipe bag of the Sioux
trimmed with beadwork

Bag for protection of
a medicine pipe, Crow

In most tribes, behavior between relatives was exactly defined. There were those with whom one was expected to joke and rough-house—who might be the same ones whose duty included the rebuke—and those with whom one dealt always in terms of great respect. In some tribes, a beautiful relationship was maintained between brothers and sisters. Brothers felt great responsibility for sisters; sisters, in turn, did their brothers many favors such as making especially fine moccasins for them. When they grew up, an extreme form of respect was required, under which they could barely speak to each other. This did not mean coldness; it showed the lofty and strong nature of their feeling for each other. Mutual service and help continued through life, and according to all accounts, the feeling of affection also continued to be very strong.

The Plains "societies," similar to those of the farming tribes west of the Mississippi, are curious. Some tribes had both men's and women's societies, others only men's. Some were purely religious, like the Crow Tobacco Society which planted the sacred tobacco

Generosity was a widespread Indian trait, both to the poor of the tribe and to peaceful visitors. Below is Catlin's painting of the feast given him and his party by the Sioux

"Dog Soldier Dance," by the modern Cheyenne artist Dick West. In the foreground sit the drummers and singers, and on either side of them a pair of women with rattles dance a quiet step. The Dog Society members put on a dance of lively character. The dancer on the extreme right is wearing the same type of headgear as the Mandan dancer shown on page 81

and held rituals connected with the plant for the good of the tribe. Others were primarily military with religious overtones, as were the Dog Societies of the Mandans and a number of northern Plains tribes. Many writers about the West refer to "Dog Soldiers" or use terms similar to it. By this is meant the members of the Dog—sometimes the Kit-Fox—Society. These men often performed the police functions, and were pledged to extreme heroism in war.

Where they were most fully developed the men's societies had a unique age grading. Young warriors, desiring to confirm their standing, would come to the members of a society of slightly older men and try to buy their insignia, songs, rituals, and privileges. After much bargaining the deal would be made. The older group would then buy out the next older club, and so on up until the oldest, having sold out, retired from the honors and activities of society membership.

Intangibles such as these were far more valuable than material possessions. Anyone who amounted to anything practiced openhanded generosity in a conspicuous manner. Chiefs often reduced themselves almost to poverty by helping the poor. What we think of as property was thought of slight consequence. But powerful songs, sacred bundles, or the knowledge of how to conduct a particular rite were valuable. Even when a man's own parents possessed some kind of sacred property, if the man wanted to receive it, he would have to buy it with horses, robes, and other goods.

Religion, much like that of the Western Farmers, was strongly shamanistic, but there were some large rituals and many minor ones that required men with priestly training. The Plains Indians and their nearer eastern neighbors developed the concept of visions dramatically. Magical-religious power, the gift of healing which made the true "medicine man," and the authority for making a sacred bundle came from visions. A vision might be the reason for starting or for calling off or for taking part in a war party. Women, also, could have visions, although they were primarily a man's business.

Visions were so important that without one a man could hardly function. At various ages, usually in the late teens, young men went to seek their visions, riding out alone, fasting, often cutting off a joint of a finger or otherwise mutilating themselves as a sacrifice or to win the pity of the spirits. They had heard many descriptions of visions, been reared on the myths about the sacred beings and how they behaved. Hunger, loneliness, pain, and intense expectation led most of them, in the end, to have a dream experience that fitted the general pattern and told the seeker that from then on his friend, his adoptive father, was a spirit elk, a buffalo, a whirlwind, or whatever it might be.

From his patron he received, or believed he received, a few prayers. His vision showed him what objects to put together as a charm that would protect him and bring him a good life. A very strong vision, or series of visions, might show that a man was intended to take up some part of religious practice. Visions could teach him new rites and prayers. A man who was unable to obtain any vision at all could buy the use of the vision and "medicine" of someone who had been especially blessed. The successful dreamer would teach him his songs or prayers and permit him to copy his charms.

As a result of the vision pattern, almost everyone had a sort of cult or sub-religion of his own inside the general religion. The rituals relating to a man's own "medicine" or to his sacred bundle were held in his own lodge before small audiences. Many of the rituals of the religious and military societies were also semi-private, and many of them, too, had their origin in visions.

Blackfeet medicine man, painted by Paul Kane. He is carrying a resplendently decorated sacred pipe

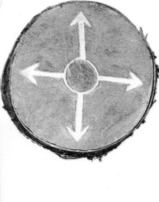

Sioux dance shield and (below) drum. Both are painted on buffalo hide

Comanche medicine gourd rattle with handle that has been beaded. It was used in a peyote ritual

Chiefs of the Blackfeet, Sarsi, and Blood tribes, painted by Paul Kane

Sioux bear dance, usually given for several days before going out on a bear hunt. The tribe's chief medicine man is the one who is wearing the complete bear's costume

Pencil and crayon drawing of a Plains dance drawn by Making Medicine, a Cheyenne, in 1875, while a prisoner at Fort Marion, Florida. In style, this drawing closely resembles the picture on the Kiowa robe shown on page 127

137

"Sun Dance," a painting by a modern Indian showing the Cheyenne-Arapaho version of this great ceremony. The artist has clearly shown the Indians' outlook on the dance, that what shocked the missionaries was beautiful and holy to the Indians

Blackfeet medicine man and (right) a Blackfeet woman with the headdress worn in the Sun Dance

In addition, there were public rituals that affected the whole tribe and also provided it with entertainment. War and scalp dances and ceremonies to bring the buffalo involved many people directly and were observed by all. One of the most important, followed in some form by almost all the Plains tribes, is called by us the Sun Dance. It is a poor name, since the dance involved little if any sun worship. Among some tribes it was a yearly fixture. Other tribes, such as the Crow, held it only rarely. Usually it was sponsored by someone who had made a vow to do so in return for supernatural help. It was a means of having powerful visions and of bringing good to the whole tribe.

Its central feature was dancing in an enclosed area, around or facing a pole made from a tree that had been "killed" and felled with great ceremony. The dancing was grave and extremely simple. It was a mark of Plains Indian ritual dancing that the dancers hardly moved from where they started. As a rule the "sun" dancers went without food or water through the whole time of their performance, which often lasted until they fell into a trance and had a vision. In some tribes, such as the Sioux, they made a sacrifice and demonstrated their courage by a form of self-torture. Two parallel slits were cut in their skin. Between the slits, underneath the skin, was run a stick, from which a string led to the central pole or to a buffalo skull. The idea was to keep jerking against the string until the strip of skin tore out. Other tribes, such as the Kiowa, who had a highly developed Sun Dance, did not practice such torture.

The Sun Dance became the principal ceremony of the Utes, a mountain people under strong Plains influence. They added to it certain features of their own culture, such as lines of men and women dancing opposite each other.

Allegedly because of the self-torture, the Sun Dance was forbidden by the U. S. Bureau of Indian Affairs about 1910. In those days, in flagrant violation of the Constitution, the Bureau lent itself readily to efforts to suppress Indian religions. The Sun Dance was forbidden whether or not the tribe practiced the torture. The Indians' right to religious freedom was not recognized until 1934, after which some of the tribes revived the dance in modified form.

Plains Indian religion was a curious mixture consisting largely of primitive thinking and a good deal of poetry. It was capable of evolving to much higher levels, and many of the more learned priests developed lofty philosophies. Black Elk, a famous Oglala Sioux priest, taught doctrines of such interest and with so much poetic and high religious content that his teachings were made the subject of two books by white men, one a poet, the other a student of comparative religions.

It was great good luck that among the first white men to go among the Plains Indians and their close neighbors were George Catlin, the American artist, and the naturalist Prince Maximilian of Wied with the artist Karl Bodmer in his party. Going out in the early 1830's, they recorded a good deal of the culture at its full peak and while direct contact with white men was still rare.

The new tribes began pushing into the High Plains in the 1720's; 1730 makes a handy, round date for the beginning of the Plains way of life as we think of it, that gallant, colorful mixture largely derived from the Western Farmers and based upon the horses and the weapons that white men had brought. Shortly after 1800, the Plains culture was at its height.

Sioux ceremonial, painted by Catlin. The candidate will receive lifelong honor and respect if he can remain standing from sun-up to sunset without fainting or falling

139

Chief Roman Nose of the Cheyenne

The Plains Indians put up a strong but losing battle with the increasing numbers of white men. Roman Nose was killed in battle in 1868; the other two chiefs below played large roles in Custer's defeat

Chief Gall of the Hunkpapa Teton Sioux

Chief Red Horn Bull of the Oglala Sioux

It died away almost as fast as it developed. By 1850, routes from the East to the growing settlements of the Pacific Coast ran through the High Plains north and south. The tribes knew no reason why foreigners should trespass on their land, kill game, build forts, even settle without permission. They raided the intruders and the intruders struck back with armies. In 1862 the Sioux carried out a series of massacres of settlers in Minnesota. The day after Christmas, 1862, thirty-eight of the leaders were hanged. The Sioux were beginning to feel the strength of "Washington."

There were minor wars and then treaties. Gold was found in the sacred Black Hills of the Sioux, so their treaty went out the window and war flamed. In the East, a great demand developed for buffalo robes. In those days, in winter, people went about in sleighs or unheated wagons and buffalo robes were ideal to keep out the cold. The buffalo hunters appeared, professional killers who slaughtered the herds from a distance with .50 calibre rifles, solely for their skins. The wholesale, wildly wasteful destruction of the animals profoundly shocked and angered the Indians.

They fought, and soon learned that they confronted an enemy armed with overwhelming weapons, great in numbers, thorough in killing. That enemy had leaders, such as Generals Crook, Howard, and Miles, who fought and dealt honorably with Indians. It also had other officers such as Colonel Custer (commonly called "General"). In 1868 Custer was in trouble with both the military authorities and the public for various failures and misdeeds. He chose to win a new reputation by raiding a series of entirely peaceful villages, killing men, women, and children. In 1876, Sitting Bull was leading the last great resistance to the white men. Custer came upon a large Indian village on the Little Big Horn River, that, as it happened, was manned by a vastly superior force of Sioux and Cheyennes who had just defeated a thousand men under General Crook. Custer sent a small force of men ahead under Major Reno—enough to alert the Indians to his presence. Then he blindly led his cavalry to the attack. He and all his men were killed. Oddly enough, this deadly display of stupidity in the Battle of the Little Big Horn finally made him a hero, a title he ill deserved.

The victory was one of the last great flares of Indian power. One by one the tribes were broken. A great many were concentrated in Oklahoma, which was still thought of as territory that no one would want. Some, like the various Sioux tribes and the Crows, received reservations in parts of their own country. The buffalo were wiped out in a few years by the white man's commercial hunting, leaving the Indians starving until the government issued them rations enough to keep them on the edge of life. Cattle ranchers took over the once free Plains. (Later, many of the cattle ranchers in turn felt much as the Indians did when farmers pre-empted the public domain and fenced it in.)

The fighting tribes did not give in easily. There were uprisings, raids of hunger and desperation. Briefly they had known a wonderful life and started a culture that might have evolved greatly had it been given time. They tried to hold to that life against hopeless odds. When everything seemed darkest, the new Ghost Dance religion, described on page 190, gave them a flicker of new hope. On December 15, 1890, Sitting Bull was killed in a struggle with Indian police on the Pine Ridge reservation. The news

Sitting Bull, leader and organizer of the Sioux

A late stage in the Battle of the Little Big Horn. Custer's cavalry has dismounted and is trying to fight off the Indians who are circling around them on the attack

Courtesy John S. du Mont

An early U.S. outpost in the Plains country, Fort Laramie, Wyoming. Forts like this one served as trade centers, and it was a considerable time before the Indians discovered that they were actually Trojan horses

spread fast. On December 22nd, a band of Sioux, all Ghost Dance followers, under a chief named Big Foot, returning to their reservation, camped under a strong cavalry guard at Wounded Knee. A battery of quick-firing Hotchkiss cannons was trained on the camp. The next day, the soldiers started to disarm the Indians and someone—probably a Sioux, but it is not sure—started shooting. The cannons opened rapid fire with explosive shells, the soldiers moved in. Sixty soldiers, two hundred Sioux men, women, and children were killed or wounded in a few moments. That was the Battle of Wounded Knee and the end of everything.

Indians and whites mingled together inside such "trading posts" as Fort Laramie

A mounted Indian scout peers across the snowy northern Plains to identify whoever has made camp. The painting is by Frederic Remington, probably the most widely known of all the painters who depicted the Old West

Sitting Bull as he looked shortly before his death

Very early soapstone killer whale of the Gabrieleño tribe

Behind the Shining Mountains

Pomo woman weaving a large "mush bowl" basket. The Pomos are among the world's finest makers of baskets

The first frontiersmen, crossing the Plains, saw the snow-capped peaks facing the rising sun and called them the Shining Mountains. Duller men later named them the Rockies. They are the northern part of the chain of mountains that forms the backbone of the Americas. Between them and the true deserts along the edge of the Southwest lies the land that received nothing of the higher cultures that trace back to the civilizations of Mexico.

Throughout this vast area, the lines between different ways of life were never sharp. The tribes in northwestern Arizona planted corn. The Utes, well within the high mountain country, had a culture that borrowed a great deal from the Plains. The Shoshones and their close relatives stretched across the north, through Wyoming, northern Utah, and southern Idaho; those on the east made trips to hunt buffalo, had grass enough to graze a fair number of horses, lived in good-sized tepees, were trying hard to be Plains Indians, and were doing pretty well at it. Those who were living at the western end were poverty-stricken desert dwellers.

144

The "Devil's Cornfield," a view of Death Valley, California. The afternoon sun makes the plants resemble corn, but there the resemblance ends. In this unproductive land where food crops cannot be raised, the California Indians survived on what roots and seeds they could find, and on small mammals, occasional deer, and even insects

Usually anthropologists separate this great region into three areas: the Great Basin, the Plateau, and California. Throughout it were peoples who spoke many languages. There were considerable differences in mode of life. All these peoples, however, excepting a few at the border of the Southwest, had in common that they did no farming, and almost all shared the same basic cultural elements, untrammeled by any Mexican influence.

The lower country in the middle of the area is called the Great Basin. Twenty thousand years ago, when the early men were drifting down into the continent, this Basin contained sixty-eight large lakes. A thousand years ago there was enough water left to enable farming and Pueblo culture to spread far into it. Now that is ended. It is a formidable, frightening country to see, except where modern irrigation has subjugated it.

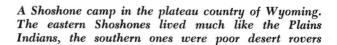

A Shoshone camp in the plateau country of Wyoming. The eastern Shoshones lived much like the Plains Indians, the southern ones were poor desert rovers

The people who lived in this desert and near-desert mostly spoke languages of the Uto-Aztecan family, languages fairly closely related to Ute, Comanche, and Hopi. They had little else in common, however, with other Uto-Aztecan Indians. They spent most of their energy simply keeping alive. There was no room, in their endless struggle, for fancy cultural items; they stuck to what was useful and they lived in a land where many white men have died.

In the western deserts, the Pah-Utes and their relatives could maintain only a "gathering" culture, one devoted to the gathering of everything edible. Most Indians know all the edible plants in their region, even though usually they don't bother with them. In many parts of the dry, Southwestern country there is a tiny potato—at least it tastes like a potato—attached to some insignificant leaves aboveground. Even today a Navaho, sitting and talking, may idly dig one up and chew on it; the true desert people hunted them painstakingly. They dug for all kinds of roots, for which reason early white men called them "Diggers." They harvested the seeds of wild grasses —which was how the planting of wheat, corn, and other grains began. In this environment, however, the practice could lead to no farming.

They also hunted, for such game as there was. A group of men would spend days, if necessary, running down a deer, a large animal and one seldom seen. Where there were antelope, the scattered groups would assemble once a year for a great drive, in which the swift beasts were driven into a brush corral and killed. Then for a short time everyone feasted on red meat, and with so many camped in one place, there could be something like ceremonies, or at least dancing that was fun, and social life.

They hunted prairie dogs, pocket gophers, and rabbits, and were not above mice. They often caught rabbits and birds by driving them into great nets, some of which were eight by thirty feet. They also hunted grasshoppers. They dug trenches into which they drove the insects, which they roasted.

A sizable family could use up the food within several miles of its camp in a short time. Then it had to move on. As a result, the people lived in scattered groups. Their dwellings were simple wickeyups, the minimum necessary shelters of brush. So narrow was the margin of life that, in most of the desert sections, very old people who could no longer move with the camp were left to die. An enclosure would be built, if possible by a spring, the ancient would be furnished with a blanket and a little food, and left. Sick infants were sometimes abandoned, also. This was not cruelty or heartlessness; it was dire necessity.

Under such circumstances, non-material culture was extremely simple. Throughout the whole region —Basin, Plateau, and California—true tribes were

147

Pah-Utes wearing buckskin shirts, photographed in 1872 near the Grand Canyon, where deer were plentiful. The kneeling men are making a fire with a twirling stick

Power came through dreams and visions, but there was no fancy business here of the vision quest. If you had a significant dream in the night, there it was; if not, you went without.

Mythology was equally simple, consisting mostly of tales about magical animals who had a hand in shaping the world, but lacking any real account of an origin of the world or of mankind. These tales are often dull to our taste, inclined to be humorous, and sometimes coarse. They are what tired people might tell at the end of a long, hard day, in the short time between eating and falling asleep.

There was a popular ceremony in which both men and women danced in a circle around a tree, singing songs about animals. The practice of men and women dancing together seems to have been a part of the Basin pattern which spread later both to the Southwest and the Plains. From the Basin also may have come the fear of the dead which required the burning of a dead man's house, forbiddance of using his name, and other observances largely intended to prevent the ghost from coming along to live with its relatives and friends. This fear still exists in strong form among the Navahos and some of the Apaches, and is one item of evidence that some of them must have passed through the Basin area on their way to the Southwest.

The Southwest is a land with an abundance of usable clay and stone, which is reflected in the housing. Its people raised cotton and wore woven garments. The Plains was above all a land of skins and hides. Habitations were made of hides, clothing of skins; ingenious uses of both run all through the culture. The Basin, on the other hand, was a land of sticks, grasses, and the kinds of trees one finds in a dry country. The people dressed in garments of grass and shredded bark, and also wove in a crude way, working strips of rabbit skin through a warp of string to form a warm robe.

Basketry and net-making were practiced extensively. Nets were important for catching small game, and basketry was used for many things. The Pah-Utes in the south made extraordinarily fine basketry and it may have been from them that the Navahos and Apaches learned their art.

Women made basket hats. Cooking was done in baskets, by the process called "stone boiling." Stones were heated red hot and then dropped into a basket full of water, bringing it to a boil. This method was common wherever the Indians had to cook without fireproof pots. The Plains Indians did the same thing, except that their containers were the carefully

hard to find except at the edges, or after the deadly pressure of the white men forced the people in desperation to unite. Instead of tribes, there were mostly groups of people who spoke alike, held the same beliefs, and recognized a common relationship. Under favorable circumstances, these people could gather once a year or so, as for the antelope hunt; otherwise each family stayed by itself. While there were recognized wise men, sometimes called "talkers," to whose advice the tribe listened, there were seldom real chiefs.

There were no clans. There was almost no organization at all. Similarly, religion was pared down to the simplest shamanism. A man who had been inspired by dreams took up healing by means of magic, or was considered to have the power to insure a successful deer hunt, or a good supply of grasshoppers. Such people commanded a certain amount of respect, but their rewards were small, and a medicine man who lost a number of patients might be killed.

cleaned stomachs of buffaloes. Some of the Basin basketry and network look very much like the ancient Basketmaker products. Probably the Basin people inherited some of the early Basketmaker culture as it was before those people learned to farm and, because their environment would not let them change, preserved it.

Human beings can become used to any kind of life and even find beauty in it. The Eskimo produces poetry about his frozen homeland; plainsmen all over the world, on steppe, pampa, or plain, learn to love the fine gradations of light and shifting cloud shadow, the movement of grass in the wind, the sheer space, while mountain people despise the flat country and cling to their sky-reaching glories. The desert Basin people found goodness in their hard life, but it remains that they stayed where they were because they were few, weak, and poor. Through the summers they endured killing heat; in much of their country, their winters were a misery of brutal cold.

Early 20th century Pomo basket, plain on the inside and covered on the outside with feathers from meadow larks' breasts and from the heads of mallard ducks

Sagebrush hut, or wickeyup, built by northern Pah-Utes in southeastern California, photographed in 1903

Feathered dance hat and (below) basket, made by Pah-Utes. This tribe made excellent basketry

Other Indians looked on the desert dwellers with pity and condescension. As late as the early nineteenth century there were Pah-Utes in the western part of what is now the Navaho Reservation, the driest part of the Navaho country. The Hopis had contact with them there, and made their name a synonym for ignorance. Even today, if a Hopi starts talking about some sacred matter before an uninitiated child or a non-Hopi, someone will remark, "There is a Pah-Ute here," to warn the speaker.

Where conditions permitted, the Basin people bettered themselves. In northwestern Arizona, the Yuman-speaking Walapais did a little farming. East

Good example of the kind of beaded dress that the women of the Shoshone tribe made

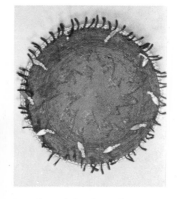

Feathered basket plaque of the Pomos. The red comes from feathers from the crest of a red-headed woodpecker, the blue from a bluebird

Ute baby carrier on a frame of basketry. Originally the sun visor simply served to shield the infant, later it was also used as decoration

of them, in a beautiful, well-watered canyon leading into the Grand Canyon from the south, their close relatives, the Havasupais, farmed actively, made good pottery, and can be classed as Southwestern.

An extension of the Basin people, both Yuman and Uto-Aztecan, reached across the hot country of southern California to the sea. In varying degrees their culture contains elements of the culture of the Southwestern Yumas. The eastern rim of the Basin is the Rocky Mountains—not country for farming, but good for hunting. Here such tribes as the Utes were strong even before the time of the horse, if the traditions of other tribes are to be believed. After the coming of the horse, they adopted a great many elements of Plains culture, although the perpendicular country they inhabited included nothing even faintly like plains. They became so warlike that they were feared even by such fighters as the Navahos.

To the north, the Basin country rises steadily, becoming the high Plateau country of Idaho, Oregon, Washington, and eastern Montana. In the Plateau country the hunting was better than it was in the desert, and the tribes on its western side had access to rivers up which came the salmon from the Pacific. A form of lily, the camas, the root of which is excellent eating, grew plentifully in many places. Here we find two new language families, Salishan and Shahaptian. In this section tribes were somewhat more organized. In the summer, the people scattered in search of food, but in winter, when a good supply of food had been stored, there were gatherings that might bring most of a tribe together.

Like the desert dwellers, the inhabitants of the Plateau were a people of basketry. They made cloth-

Man on horseback, a section of a Shoshone man's robe of painted elkskin, probably made about 1900

150

Above, Washo basket made by Dat-so-la-lee, famous for the perfection of her work. At right, a Panamint basket

Basketry hamper with lid made by the Thompson River Indians of the interior of British Columbia

ing of bark fibers and woven rabbit skin, but, with better hunting, they had considerably more buckskin. They used brush shelters, but these were often larger than the ones built in the desert, and they were often built on a gabled frame. Some of the Plateau people also covered gabled frameworks with well-woven mats. In winter many tribes lived in earth lodges.

The strength that came from visions was of vital importance to the Plateau people. Women as well as men could have them. Young men went to great lengths to obtain visions, tearing themselves with thorns, bathing in icy waters, starving. Through visions men received guardian spirits, who might return in later life to demonstrate that this man had been blessed. When such a vision was due, usually in midwinter, the man gave a public feast lasting for

Beaded bag made by the Yakimas of Washington

Beaded buckskin belt of the Walla Walla tribe of eastern Washington. It was collected between 1872-1880

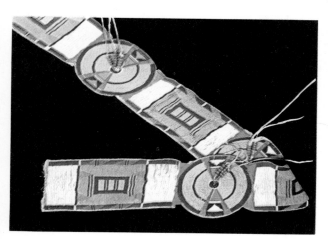

Painted rawhide dance drum made by the Modocs of northern California

151

A *Flathead woman and child painted by Paul Kane probably about 1850. The shape of the woman's head is due to intentional distortion in infancy; the child's head is bound so as to cause the same effect*

many days, in the course of which he would fall unconscious, revive, sing an inspired song which a medicine man would interpret, then dance and sing around a bonfire. Others who had been similarly blessed would perform, in their turns, the dances and songs that had been revealed to them. Every man, it seems, was something of a shaman, although only the medicine men performed rites for others.

On the whole, the Plateau people were peaceful. Most of their fighting was defensive. Taken broadly, their culture looks like Basin culture as it would have developed in more favorable surroundings.

The coming of the horse made great changes. The tribes, until then foot travelers who also used some bark and dugout canoes, became more mobile. Some pushed toward the Plains, only to be pushed back, time and again, by the Blackfeet, Sioux, and others.

Lewis and Clark meeting the Flathead Indians in Montana, painted by Charles Russell

The tent of Chief Washakie is in the foreground of this picture of a Wyoming Shoshone camp

Washakie, one of the most powerful chiefs of the eastern branch of the Shoshone throughout most of the 19th century. He and his band befriended the large numbers of white men passing through Shoshone territory. Fort Washakie, in west central Wyoming, is named after him

Many were able to engage in frequent buffalo hunting. Those tribes that could not reach the buffalo country nevertheless gained by the increased trade in such goods as shells from the sea and horses for meat and skins. The Plains ideas on war spread to the easternmost Plateau tribes. The use of tepees spread as far as the western part of the Plateau. Canoeing, on the other hand, declined.

The coastal parts of California and up into Oregon were settled by many small groups, speaking languages of many of the families already named in this

Village life of the Pomos in the early 19th century. The women in the foreground are going through various steps toward preparing acorns for bread. In the area where the Pomos lived there was plenty of small game, some deer, and acorns everywhere. Men often wore the head of a deer (as at right) as a decoy when hunting. Pomo houses were little more than brush shelters, but each village had a dance house, shown at the back, in which the single women sometimes slept in cold weather

book and two new ones, Yukian and Penutian. The region was bordered on one side by the sea, on the other by high mountains; the climate was mild and the food supply fairly good. Groups of people who were passing through stopped there, and were joined by others, who, for one reason or another, came over the mountains to seek refuge. That part of this strip south of about the fortieth meridian is the culture area known as "Californian." Its people show many characteristics of Basin culture, with varying elements from the Yuman and Pueblo branches of the Southwest, and other elements of their own. The whole situation provides a wonderful playground for scientists and specialists, but it provides only confusion for everyone else.

The California Indians had pretty decent hunting and good fishing. They developed ingenious modes of getting the varied game in their vicinity. For instance, a hunter would take a number of gourds, or other round objects, somewhat larger than his head and float them down a stream past a flock of ducks until the birds ceased to pay attention to them.

Klamath hat decorated with beadwork

Then he would float down with his head in one, and as he went by, grab a duck by the feet and pull it under water. This would not frighten the other ducks; the trick could be worked on the same flock a number of times in succession.

The Pomos were expert at making nets, which they used for catching fish, birds, and small game. Below, a small boy has removed a bird from a net held by an older man

Pomo "gift" or "jewel" basket

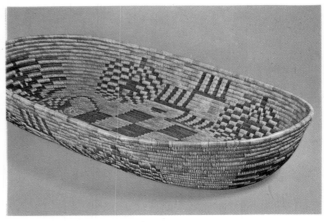

Flat-bottomed basket of the Mission Indians

Large, conical burden basket, Pomo

Vase-shaped basket, Pomo

Karok basket with lid

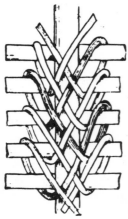

Types of stitches used by the Pomos in weaving their baskets

In the area were many oaks, the acorns of which were made into a nourishing flour. This was a staple food, but one that took some ingenuity to work out, as acorns are intolerably bitter with tannic acid. Altogether, it required six different processes—including grinding, leaching with water, drying, and roasting—before the flour could be used for gruel.

Some of the California Indians were about the finest basketweavers in America. The work is extraordinary, both for fineness of technique and excellence of design, and is often unbelievably delicate.

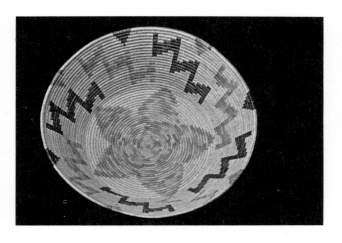

Mission Indian basket made in the 1880's

Basket hat of the Pah-Utes. Many of the people of the Basin, Plateau, and California areas made hats of this type, as did several of the tribes of the Northwest Coast

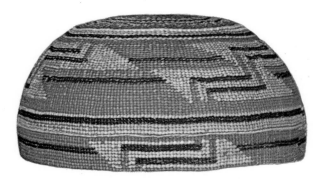

Basket hat of the Shastas

Large Klikitat basket. These people were Plateau-dwellers living in southern Washington

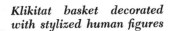

Klikitat basket decorated with stylized human figures

Basket of the Tulare tribe of California with a woven human figure design, and decorated with black feathers

Some baskets, into which brilliant, small feathers have been worked, have almost the effect of having been inlaid with jewels.

Like the northern Atlantic Coast Indians, the Californians had a form of shell money, made from shells of various kinds. They traded some of the beads westward (necklaces of such beads are highly prized by the Indians of Arizona and New Mexico even today) and used the rest among themselves. Shell money had a fairly fixed value and was used in a number of transactions.

*Dance headdresses worn by the Indians of the San Francisco area as sketched in 1814;
two of the three people are also wearing necklaces of bits of highly polished shell*

By and large, the North American Indians encouraged generosity, often of a somewhat showy kind. Such tribes as the Hopis, who knew the famine that a drought year could cause, sometimes kept a year's supply of corn laid by, but even among them there was a great deal of giving and sharing. Many of the California tribes preached the opposite—a sort of mean thrift. Amassing quantities of shell money became an end in itself.

During the summers, the California Indians stayed pretty much on the move, gathering food. The people could seldom find enough wild food in one place to stay put. The pickings were good enough, however, to enable them to live in sizable groups, and to take up a village life in winter. Tribes were pretty clearly defined; most had clans with descent traced through the father, and many of them were divided into moieties, or halves, which performed various services for each other.

The men often went naked, or wore a breechclout of skin, or wrapped skin around their waists; women wore aprons in front and behind, of shredded bark or strings. They went barefoot most of the time, but occasionally wore crudely shaped skin moccasins or sandals made of fiber. The men decorated their heads

with arrangements of bright, small feathers. They made robes out of rabbitskins. They also tied great quantities of feathers to strings and wove them into feather blankets.

In the southern part, the people built cone-shaped houses, using a framework of poles solidly covered with thatched grass often tied on roots and all. Some of these houses had smoke holes, some did not, but almost all had two small doorways opposite each other to allow for circulation of air. In the north, the houses were more solidly built, and many of them were partly underground.

The religion and ceremonies of the Californians, as might be expected, fell in between the scanty practices of the wandering desert people and the elaborate fixed rituals of the farmers. There were ceremonies for such purposes as ensuring the coming of the salmon. Some tribes had ceremonies with masked dancers, some had dancers completely disguised in feathers, that may derive from the kachinas of the Pueblos. A number of tribes made a crude kind of ground painting, suggestive of the Southwestern "sand paintings," by pouring dry colors on a circle of smoothed earth.

Where rituals are few, a good deal of attention

Looking Glass, one of the great war leaders of the Nez Percés, photographed in 1871. He was killed in 1877, taking part in Chief Joseph's retreat toward Canada

is likely to be paid to the strange things that happen when a girl becomes a woman, and similar attention may be extended to a boy's becoming a man. A very poor people, like those in the desert, cannot give too much time to such matters, while for people such as the Pueblos, with their great, elaborate rituals, these individual matters lose importance. The California tribes made a major ceremony of boys' and girls' initiations. Since they, too, felt that visions were essential to men, they insured that boys would have a vision during initiation by giving them a potent drug, a brew made from the root of the Jimson weed.

The Californians were not so much warlike as quarrelsome. Each little tribe guarded its pocket of territory jealously, and acted immediately against trespassers. One tribe, the Maidu, even kept sentries posted along its boundaries. Often, when there was serious trouble, two tribes would line up; then each would pick a champion to fight it out for the tribe.

The Mission at Santa Barbara, one of the headquarters for the California Mission Indians

strong missions. The priests gathered in the roving Indians, with no little use of force. The idea was to settle them in villages, teach them useful arts, including farming, and make them into an exploitable, Christian labor force. A good many of the wanderers found the clothes they were forced to wear stifling, the new way of life like being in prison. Some died of it; the others became accustomed to it. They did not become self-sufficient, but dependent upon the priests; they were not farmers but farm laborers.

When Mexico became independent, funds for support of the missions were cut off and most of them closed. Then the "Mission Indians" were lost. They neither knew how to survive as they had in the old days, nor how to take care of themselves in the new manner. They suffered greatly. To add to their sorrows, came the discovery of gold in 1849 and then the gold rush that filled California with white men.

After the fight, there was long consulting and haggling, ending with payments of shells, which settled the matter. Some scalps were taken, and when they were, it was not just a small piece off the top of the head, but everything, including the ears.

About half the tribes cremated their dead, as did the Southwestern Yumas, and had similar follow-up ceremonies. Often the moiety to which the deceased did not belong handled the funeral arrangements, so that the bereaved moiety was not contaminated. The house and valuable articles might be burned, including specially woven, extremely fine baskets. After the funeral rites, or a year later when a second ceremony was held, the taboo on mentioning the dead person's name was lifted. That taboo was far more troublesome for primitive tribes who named people after objects than it would be for us. If the deceased's name was "White Deer," or "Oak Leaf," for instance, a couple of words in constant use had to be dropped until in some way the taboo could be gotten around.

The Spanish occupied southern California as they did New Mexico. In California they established

Chief Joseph of the Nez Percés, one of the ablest generals that the North American Indians ever produced

The little groups were thrust aside, and even the tribes farther north were overwhelmed.

A series of treaties was negotiated by which the Indians gave up most of the country in exchange for fairly adequate reservations. Pressure from what had become the new state of California prevented the treaties from being ratified, although the Indians had moved out of the land they had surrendered. There was nothing for the unfortunate little tribes to do but drift about, scrabbling for a living as best they could. Finally pieces of land were set aside for them, usually the poorest there was. The result is a curious mess, with 116 reservations in the state, ranging in size from over 25,000 acres to 2 acres. Few of the shattered tribes could keep their culture, although some have made remarkable efforts to continue as groups and retain their identity.

At first the white men wanted only to pass through the Basin and Plateau areas, so that they troubled the Indians in those regions relatively little. Later, they began to take the land. Not many of the tribes were well enough organized to offer serious resistance. The finding of gold and silver in Nevada brought great trouble to the Indians there. Throughout, the increasing white population destroyed the narrow margin of food. Many of the desert people became hangers-on around white settlements; some did not receive title to land until the 1930's. However, the stronger tribes of the Plateau country fared somewhat better.

One group, a part of the loosely organized tribe called Nez Percé of Oregon, put up a resistance that is famous, under the leadership of a remarkable Indian called Chief Joseph. They faced an all-too-familiar situation. They had accepted a reservation peaceably. Then they agreed to cede part of it. Part was not enough; the white men wanted Chief Joseph's homeland. He and his band refused, and started fighting. They fought magnificently, but they were hopelessly outnumbered, so they decided to move to Canada where, as all Indians knew, treaties were not broken. Under Chief Joseph's generalship they conducted a fighting retreat, with their women and children accompanying them, that is considered one of the great retreats of military history.

Cold, weary, near starvation, they were caught and surrounded almost within sight of the Canadian border. Chief Joseph was offered honorable terms and he surrendered. The terms were promptly forgotten, and he and his band were shipped to Oklahoma, where many of them died in the low altitude and the heat.

No Horns on His Head, a young Nez Percé painted in 1854 or 1855. His shirt and his hair style are Siouan

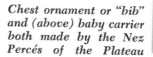

Chest ornament or "bib" and (above) baby carrier both made by the Nez Percés of the Plateau

161

Kwakiutl carved wooden figurine

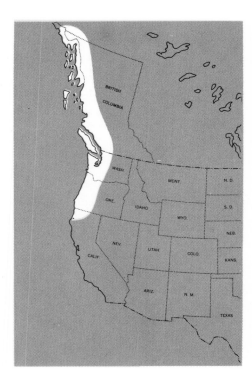

The Eagle, the Raven, and the Whale

Kwakiutl raven hat. The raven was a popular figure in Northwest Coast mythology and is often seen in its art

There is a very long, narrow strip of land between the edge of the Pacific Ocean and the mountains, beginning in the northern tip of California and running north through British Columbia and Alaska more than 1,500 miles to where the Alaskan Coast bends westward at Yakutat Bay. This region is called the Northwest Coast. The mountains are fairly high in California, high enough in Oregon to comb the clouds that constantly drift in from the ocean, causing heavy rainfall, farther north almost impassable except in a few places. In the north, also, the space between the mountains and the water is so little that even places on which to build villages are scarce.

A few big rivers cut through the mountains from the interior, such as the Columbia and the Fraser. The heavy rains make little rivers pouring down the slopes, many of which have cut deep, narrow inlets in the shore. Offshore, from the southern end of British Columbia to the northern end of the strip,

Tlingit shirt. The design painted on it represents a bear. This bear is identifiable as such by certain signs used by the Northwest Coast people, such as the large jaws and big teeth, the upright ears, and by the quite realistic claws

is a chain of islands. The climate, although wet, is not very cold, because the Japan Current warms it. With its combination of islands, river mouths, bays, and inlets, the Northwest Coast is one of the great fishing territories of the world.

The first white men found this area occupied by people having an advanced culture which is surely the strangest in North America. These people spoke languages belonging to at least five quite different families. They are usually listed by their languages, for, although the speakers of one tongue might not form one tribe and might even make war upon each other, they all shared the same special form of the general Northwest Coast culture. Counting from north to south, the main language groups were the Tlingit in Alaska, the Haida, Tsimshian, Kwakiutl in British Columbia, the Nootka in British Columbia and Washington, then the Bella Coola, Coast Salish, and Chinook, and in California the Karok, Yurok, and

After section of a Haida ceremonial canoe in the American Museum of Natural History. The figures are models, but most of the objects are the real thing. The party in the canoe is shown as on the way to a potlatch. The chief, in full regalia, stands in the stern. In front of him is a bear dancer, and farther forward, a shaman, drumming

culture came to be; Northwest Coast progress, then, was almost entirely homemade.

Then, as we have seen, advancement towards civilization comes with settling down in one place and with spare time, and this combination comes with farming. But along that coast there was no farming, except a very little planting of tobacco. Instead, there was an unlimited supply of seafood, from whales to clams; there were herring, smelt, olachen, halibut, and flounder; there were seal, porpoises, and sea lions, and above all the salmon, five varieties of which ran up the rivers by the million every year. Once the people had learned to store their catches, they had the same conditions as farmers—plenty of food on hand, no need to go wandering, and spare time to devote to things other than the struggle for existence.

In addition to the foods from the sea, there was a moderate supply of berries. In the south, the women dug the starchy camas roots. In southern Oregon and in California, the people used acorn meal, as did those of the California culture. There was some very good hunting of migratory birds, and hunting of deer, bear, mountain goats, and elk.

The people cooked by stone-boiling in watertight baskets and boxes or steaming in pits with hot stones, and by broiling. During their leisure time, among other arts, they elaborated their cookery. Around 1900, a housewife of the Kwakiutl tribe gave an

A. J. Miller's painting of a Chinook in the 1830's

Hupa, borderline peoples whose customs are almost as much Californian as Northwest Coast.

Apart from the oddities of the culture itself, two things about its very foundations are unusual. For one, all the advanced cultures we have looked at so far resulted from the influence of the civilizations of Mexico. The great deserts and mountain ranges of the Basin and Plateau lie between the Northwest Coast and any contact with those sources. There are traces of influence of an ancient, Siberian Iron Age culture. Apart from that, the Northwest Coast people were affected by Eskimos, by the Plateau people, and by the primitive, hunting Athabascans who lived in Canada behind the rugged, coastal mountains. All of these were far behind what the Northwest Coast

anthropologist 150 recipes without coming to the end of her mental cookbook.

In Oregon and California, where deer were plentiful and the fishing only moderately good, hunting land animals was important. In the north, where the fishing was superb, game rather scarce, and hunting in the steep mountains difficult, hunting was something of a luxury. Yet the northern tribes hunted mountain goats.

A modern hunter thinks himself lucky to fix that quarry in the telescopic sights of a high-powered rifle. The Northwest Coast hunters, however, were able to kill mountain goats with spears. A few men would move along the high slopes, letting the goats detect their presence enough to make them move in the direction the hunters wanted, but without really frightening them. Slowly the animals were worked downhill and into a narrow, steep gorge or other suitable place where they could be cornered. Other hunters, waiting ready, then closed in and made the kill with their spears, or perhaps with clubs.

Salmon, running up the great rivers to spawn, were dipped out with nets and caught in fish traps by the people of the Northwest Coast. Some were eaten on the spot, the rest cured and stored for later use

Interior of a Nootka house sketched by John Webber, draftsman on Captain Cook's last voyage to the South Seas, 1776-80. The huge, carved house posts in the rear were used both as decoration and as a support for the beams. Dried fish hang from the rafters

This procedure required extraordinary skill in stalking and climbing. To the Indians' mind, it also required supernatural help, so the hunt was preceded by elaborate ritual. The ritual, the right to acquire the skill, the right to use the places where the mountain goats could be trapped, were possessions. They were the property of chiefs, were jealously guarded, and were passed along by inheritance. Throughout the area, similar kinds of knowledge, rituals, and the right to use certain places were property.

It was the special right of chiefs, also, to hunt whales. The greatest whalers were the Nootkas. These men were fine coastwise seamen and boat-builders; they could turn out a seaworthy vessel more than fifty feet long.

The ritual to be performed before whaling, and by those who remained on shore while it was going on, was elaborate and exacting, for here was the most dangerous of all forms of hunting. The equipment

Nootka woman wearing a basket hat—another of the sketches done by John Webber in the late 18th century

166

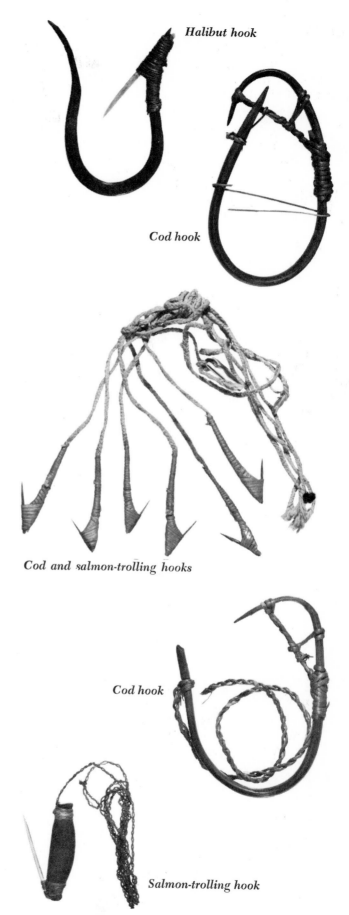

Halibut hook

Cod hook

Cod and salmon-trolling hooks

Cod hook

Salmon-trolling hook

was expensive. The chief himself was the harpooner. The line for the harpoon had to be laid on board so that it ran out without a hitch, and the arrangement was further complicated by the fact that four buoys of inflated sealskin were tied to the line at intervals. The harpoon was too heavy to throw. The whalers sneaked up right alongside of the whale, hoping that the great beast would not notice them. Then the harpooner, standing with his right foot on the gunwale, drove the harpoon home. Immediately the crew paddled for all they were worth, to break away from the whale before it could crush them. A second whaleboat, commanded by a relative of the chief, might be given the honor of putting in the second harpoon. This was driven in when the victim began to tire from dragging the line and from loss of blood.

By and by the whale would wear itself out. If it had not destroyed the whalers first, they would cut the tendons of its flukes with a chisel-like blade, which left it helpless. Then the killing lance was thrust to the heart. If all the prayers and rites had been correctly performed, the whale would have come close to the beach before its death. If there had been an error, it would have gone out to sea, and the crews might have a couple of days' paddling, towing the beast, before they landed it.

Whaling was an adventure; ordinary fishing was business, the methods ingenious and competent. The Indians used hooks and lines—the hooks made of wood, bone, and horn—spears, harpoons, dip-nets worked by one man, seines handled by crews, and various other kinds of nets and traps. Herring was also taken with a "herring rake," a paddlelike board with teeth along one side of the blade. When the herring were running, two men would go out in a canoe, one paddling, the other using the rake. He would swing this through the water much in the manner of a paddle, the teeth to the rear. At each swing he hit and spiked one or more herring, which he flipped into the boat.

The Northwest Coast people were not seafarers as, for instance, the Polynesians were. They did not use sails until after contact with white men, and although some of them made coastwise voyages of a hundred miles or more, they hated to lose sight of land. Still, they were supremely at home in their canoes. If a man in a canoe came across an animal such as a deer, elk, or bear, swimming, he would

Haida slate carving—dogs and a hunter rescue a woman from a bear

Tlingit wooden tobacco mortar carved to represent a bird

Tlingit wooden grease dish shaped like a seal

catch up with it and beat it over the head with his paddle until, also with his paddle, he could shove its head under water and drown it. Then he would haul it on board.

Fish made up one element on which the Northwest Coast people built their culture. The other important element was wood. All along the coast trees were plentiful, in particular the great evergreens—spruce, fir, yew, and redwood in the south, and best of all, the easily workable cedar. Canoes were hollowed out of wood, solid houses built of wood, utensils of all sorts were of wood. Cedar bark was made into yarn and woven into clothing. Mats were made of bark. A baby's cradle might be made of wood and lined with bark, pounded and worked into a padding as soft as cotton. Among other articles of wood were masks, chests, boxes, bowls, spoons, rattles, and, of course, the famous totem poles. There were few tricks of woodworking the people did not know. They carved wood, painted it, steamed and bent it, fitted it, and inlaid it with shell, mica,

Painted Kwakiutl carving of a beaver biting his tail. The cross-hatchings on the tail identify it as a beaver

Nootka cradle. The decorations include a killer whale, head turned backwards and tail turned toward the head, and a wolf. The human face at right may be a "filler"

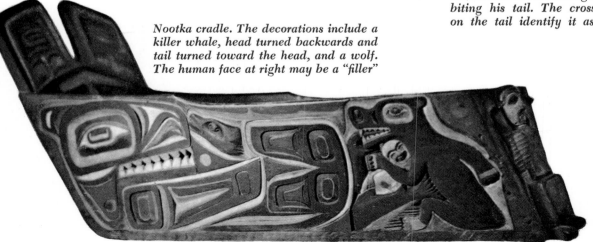

and copper. The chisels, adzes, and knives they used in their woodworking mostly had blades of sharp, strong shell since workable stone was scarce. They did have a few iron tools probably from Siberia.

As well as having some iron, the people had a little copper, acquired by trade with Indians in the subarctic Canadian regions, where there was free copper. As in other parts of the New World where this metal could be obtained, it was regarded as precious. In the Northwest Coast, it was beaten into sheets of various sizes, called "coppers," which were highly valued. It was also worked into knife blades. Copper is a soft metal to be put to this kind of use, but by hammering it when it is cold, it can be given enough temper to make it serviceable.

With their skill at working woods, the people naturally evolved the art of carving, which they carried over to horn. They also did a little stone carving. In the nineteenth century, after they became familiar with white men's tools, they developed a fine technique in carving slate.

Niska headdress of shell-inlaid wood

Haida dishes carved from slate and inlaid with shell or ivory. The circular decorations on two of them were modeled on designs learned from the Russians

Salish hand adze, wood with steel blade, with a carved wolf's head for decoration

Tlingit tobacco mortar. Its head is that of a seal, but it seems to have a bird's tail

Totem poles are well known Northwest Coast items; this one is from Prince Rupert Island

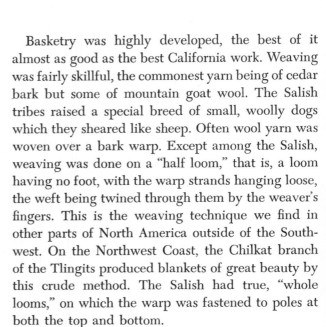

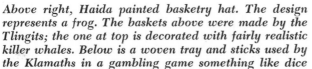

Above right, Haida painted basketry hat. The design represents a frog. The baskets above were made by the Tlingits; the one at top is decorated with fairly realistic killer whales. Below is a woven tray and sticks used by the Klamaths in a gambling game something like dice

Basketry was highly developed, the best of it almost as good as the best California work. Weaving was fairly skillful, the commonest yarn being of cedar bark but some of mountain goat wool. The Salish tribes raised a special breed of small, woolly dogs which they sheared like sheep. Often wool yarn was woven over a bark warp. Except among the Salish, weaving was done on a "half loom," that is, a loom having no foot, with the warp strands hanging loose, the weft being twined through them by the weaver's fingers. This is the weaving technique we find in other parts of North America outside of the Southwest. On the Northwest Coast, the Chilkat branch of the Tlingits produced blankets of great beauty by this crude method. The Salish had true, "whole looms," on which the warp was fastened to poles at both the top and bottom.

In addition to woven goods, these people had pounded bark and many kinds of skins and furs from which to make clothing. Immediately north and west of them were the Eskimos, who, following Arctic tradition, covered themselves from head to foot with beautifully tailored garments, but the Northwest Coast people did not copy them. In warm weather men went naked unless they had reason to wear the insignia of their rank. Women wore bark skirts. In cold and wet weather, robes or capes, often of shredded cedar bark, and a basket hat gave protection. They knew how to make moccasins, but often went barefoot even in snow and apparently did not mind. The Chilkats copied a one-piece trousers-and-moccasins outfit from the Athabascans of the interior with whom they traded. It looked like a fisherman's waders or a small child's pyjama trousers. They also copied fringed buckskin shirts decorated with porcupine quill embroidery.

Salish women weaving, an interior by the mid-19th century artist Paul Kane

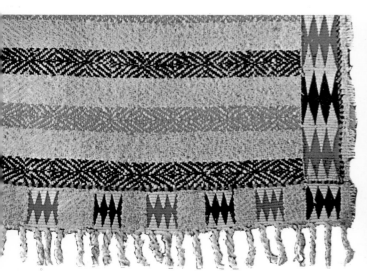

Salish chief's blanket made of mountain goat's wool

Salish blanket woven with wool and vegetable fibers

Blanket of mountain goat wool and cedar bark fiber woven by the Chilkat division of the Tlingit tribe

171

Tlingit painted wooden box drum. It has an eagle portrayed on it, as shown by the turned-down beak and the wings. The lower face may be that of a sea monster

The club below is of the type called a "slave killer" and was intended for exactly that purpose. During a potlatch, it was not uncommon for a slave or two to be killed as a mark of the chief's ability to buy more. This particular club was made sometime before 1900 by the Kwakiutls who lived around Alert Bay, British Columbia. The eyes and teeth of inlaid shell give it a fierce appearance

Much of Northwest Coast dressing was intended to show rank rather than to give protection from the weather. If anything, display counted for more than comfort.

The tribes from the Nootka in Washington northward were definitely warlike; those to the south might be described as quarrelsome and not afraid of a fight. After trade with the white men began, the tribes often suffered from the piratical conduct of many of the seafarers who came to deal with them. They did not hesitate, in retaliation, to attack the next ship that came along. In 1799 the Russians established a fort in Tlingit territory near Sitka; three years later, the Tlingits wiped it out. As late as 1852, the Chilkats sent an expedition three hundred miles inland to destroy a fortified Hudson's Bay Company post, because until the post was established, they had enjoyed a monopoly of trade with the Indians of that area. They behaved remarkably humanely, turning the people they captured loose with a strong warning to stay out of the region.

From the Nootkas north there was true warfare, waged to wipe out another tribe. There was none of the game of courting danger and winning honors we find from the Southeast to the Plains. War had a purpose, arising from the fact that here was one of the few places in North America where the population was rather crowded and land became valuable. Good village sites, the best fishing places, were in demand. War creates warlike habits. Villages with increasing populations could desire to wipe out a neighbor, even one of the same group.

South of the Nootka, the fighting was mostly brought about by feuds, to avenge a slain man. Vengeance brought countervengeance. Feuds were ended by payment of indemnities for the man killed. Deaths on opposite sides did not cancel each other out. Instead, each one was subject to long haggling. Among the groups in California, the worth of a slain man was the amount of shell money paid as his mother's bridal price.

Similar feuds occurred in the north, also. Among those warlike people, it was sometimes impossible to come to an agreement on the price that was to be paid for the killing of a man of importance. For the good of the village, a chief or noble related to the killer, and of approximately the same rank as the

done so that the chief might be accompanied by others or, as some said, that others might be in mourning, too.

Weapons included bows, a variety of clubs and spears, and, for in-fighting, an efficient knife with a long, heavy blade and a second, short blade fastened to the upper end of the handle. Some of the big war canoes were built with a high shield at the bow, pierced for archery. This made a useful type of landing craft for beach operations. The Northwest Coast Indians also used armor. Helmets were made of wood, and usually were carved into horrifying faces. Slats strung together were wrapped around the body, or cuirasses of heavy hide were worn.

victim, might offer himself. He put on his finest regalia with his highest insignia, and came from his house to the enemy dancing a stately dance that was part of his inheritance. If the other side had good manners, it would wait until he had come close to the warriors before killing him.

There was also, in the north, simple raiding, one of the main purposes of which was to capture slaves. There was not much need for slaves in that economy, but having a few around the house showed that a chief was either a successful war leader or rich enough to buy an expensive article. Also, in the lavish ceremonials called potlatches, a fine way to show off one's wealth and prodigality was to have a slave killed, using for the purpose the proper weapon, which was called a "slave killer."

Among many tribes, when an important chief died, the tribe felt called upon to stage a raid. This was

Tlingit wooden helmet and armor of slats that were wrapped around the body. Such helmets were worn over a wooden collar that would take up the force of a blow and protect the neck from injury. The warlike face was almost certainly intended to strike fear into the enemy

173

Wildman mask, depicting an old legend in which a man is made to lose his wits by being bitten by land otters

Carved and painted mask, Kwakiutl, of a sea monster with a hawk's head

Carved and painted mask representing the face of a man, made by the Bella Coolas of Nishka, British Columbia

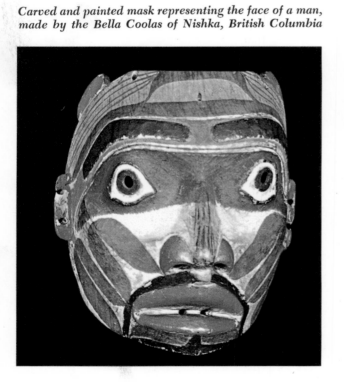

Salish mask, man with hawk's beak, of a man transformed into a bird

Wooden fool mask with painted face made by the Tsimshians and worn at a potlatch in 1912

174

Tlingit Bear Chief's clan hat. On ceremonial occasions the chief would wear this hat to prove his membership in the Bear Clan. The subdivisions rising above the hat give his rank, in the same manner as sergeant's stripes

Carved and painted wooden mask made by the Haidas

Wooden mask of a man's face made by the Kwakiutls

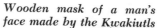

The masks and Bear Chief's hat on these pages give some idea of the variety of the Northwest Coast art, ranging all the way from moderate realism to fantasy. The two masks at the bottom of the page on the left well represent men with painted faces, above them is a being who is a human and a hawk at the same time, and in the upper left-hand corner a fine portrayal of a man who has lost his wits. The chief's bear does not look like one, nor does it need to. Skill, imagination, perception, and conventionalized designs blend in a variety of ways to make a real art

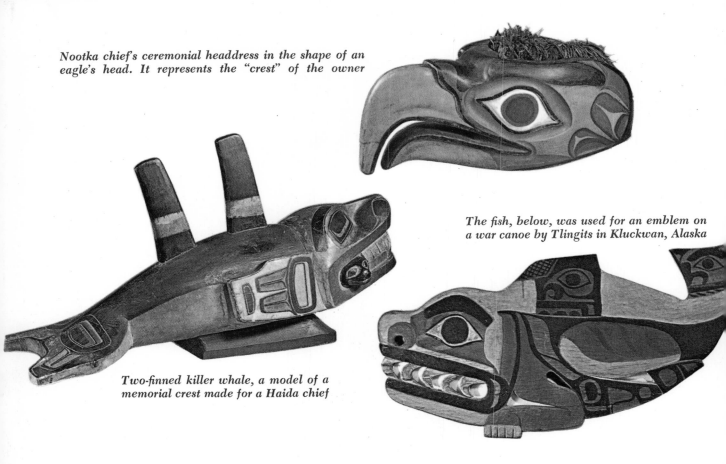

Nootka chief's ceremonial headdress in the shape of an eagle's head. It represents the "crest" of the owner

The fish, below, was used for an emblem on a war canoe by Tlingits in Kluckwan, Alaska

Two-finned killer whale, a model of a memorial crest made for a Haida chief

Throughout the Northwest Coast, social organization and religion were closely interwoven. Each village was an independent unit. Each one might make war with other villages of the same language and customs, or might be loosely allied with some of them. Villages were built up around a core of closely related people. In the north there were clans, with descent traced through the mother. In the south, many groups traced descent, as we do, through both father and mother but with emphasis on the father's line. Inheritance, which was of vital importance, was traced in the same way as descent. Where the clan system obtained, the village was organized around the clan. Common clan names were Eagle, Raven, Wolf, and Blackfish, the last name referring to both the killer whale and the black whale. Some villages were also divided into moieties, or halves.

In the north, no matter how the group was organized, there were within it lines of descent, or lineages, of different rank. The highest of these traced their descent back to a supernatural animal, such as a Raven, Eagle, or Bear, or to a human who had received special powers and rights from an experience with a supernatural being. The ancestry of an individual as well as supernatural experiences or unusual achievements—on his part or on the part of an ancestor—gave him the right to certain insignia, or "crests." Some of these crests were carved on totem poles. From ancestry, supernatural experiences, and also by purchase came what the Indians considered as possessions. These included such things as the right to dance certain dances, sing certain songs, perform certain rituals, fish in the salmon-catching areas, and

Rattles carved in the shape of a bird were common on the Northwest Coast. This one represents a merganser, a species of duck, carrying four young on her back. It was carved by the Tlingits and was used by a shaman

hunt whales. In the south, the hereditary principle was weaker; possessions were passed along more by purchase than by inheritance.

Out of the variety of crests, rights, and prerogatives developed a detailed system of grading—from chiefs, who had a great deal, down through the nobility to the common people, the poorest of whom had no special rights at all. Below them were the slaves.

Anything owned by an individual, whether commoner, noble, or chief, was not entirely his own. It was also the property of the group as a whole, gave them status as compared to other groups, and worked to their benefit. Thus, when a chief was called upon to give a great feast to the chiefs and notable men of another group, everybody pitched in to help and contribute. In due course, the chief paid them all back.

Religion was clearly based on shamanism but with many elaborations. The usual magical tricks by which shamans proved their power were developed into highly theatrical devices. Supernatural figures came flying down the smoke hole of the house; a magician was put into a wooden box, the box burned, and the magician reappeared unharmed; speaking tubes of kelp enabled performers to make voices sound from strange parts of the building. Many major ceremonies were held by firelight inside the great houses. This made deceptions easy, since such details as the fine strings that made masks open or by which objects were made to fly through the air, could not be seen.

Shamanism is closer to magic than to religion. The shift to formal religion usually hinges on some event of vivid importance to the people, generally one that recurs at regular intervals, often one concerning the people's major food supply. In the Southwest in early July everyone waited for the rain with intense anxiety. To leave the bringing of it to a few specialists would have been emotionally impossible; everyone wanted to help.

The important event on the Northwest Coast was the yearly return of the various spawning fish, especially the salmon. Salmon hatch far up the rivers. As small, unsalmonlike fish called parr, they swim down the rivers and disappear into the sea. After a number of years, when they are full-grown, these creatures return to the exact place where they were spawned, spawn in their turn, and kill themselves doing so.

Family staff of a Tlingit chief with his crests. It was customary for a chief to carry a staff like this at ceremonies or potlatches to indicate his importance

Tlingit food box made out of a single piece of red cedar. The design represents a sea serpent

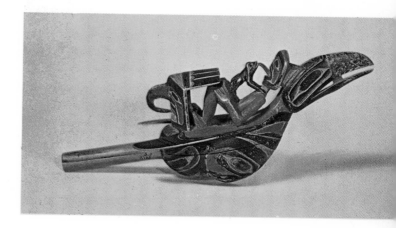

Raven rattle of a type made by the Tsimshians and the Tlingits, and later by other groups. The figure on the raven's back is a shaman holding a frog on his knees. Frogs were thought to give additional power to shamans

177

Tlingit ceremonial "button blanket," made of a regular Hudson's Bay blanket with red broadcloth trim, decorated with buttons forming the shape of a killer whale

The Indians saw the salmon running up the rivers each year. They saw those that reached the high waters die there. They did not associate the parr with the salmon. They came to the conclusion that these fish were immortal. The fish swam voluntarily into the rivers to feed mankind (and bears), died, and were reborn in the ocean. Here was something that called for major ritual in order to keep it going. It also called for great care in returning all salmon skeletons intact to the water. The ritual involved everybody, but particularly the chiefs who owned the fishing grounds.

In the office of chief there was a curious blend of religious rights and duties, inherited rank, and wealth. To show his position, the chief sought to exhibit his crests—the marks of his rank—in every possible way. This display, combined with the general reverence for divine members of such species of animals as killer whale, raven, bear, beaver, and wolf, and for such mythical creatures as the thunderbird, shaped an art.

Over and over again these animals and the experiences connected with them are represented in Northwest Coast art. Some of the work was simple and realistic. Often it was fantastically elaborated for the sake of decorative effects. The artists had a tendency to cover every inch of the object they were decorating. To do this, they would fill in any blank space with a face or a minor figure that had nothing to do with the main subject. Sometimes they would use small eyes to mark the joints of an animal or as space fillers to cover blank areas.

Kwakiutl double mask carved out of wood. When the outer part is closed, it represents a raven; when open, a human face appears inside. It was worked by strings

It was common to show an animal as if it had been split down the back, one side extending to the right, one to the left. The head might also be split and shown as two profiles touching each other, or might be handled full face.

The body might have no resemblance to the original, and you could identify the animal only by some detail, such as the eagle's hooked beak, the killer whale's big teeth and sharklike fin, or the beaver's chisel-like front teeth and scaly tail. It sounds

Tlingit silver bracelet with a shark split down the back

The bear design on this Chilkat man's shirt is to a large extent made up of small faces. A row of faces forms the teeth; three other faces make up the long, outstretched tongue

Haida dance shirt made of a Hudson's Bay blanket decorated with a red flannel bear, made sometime before 1891

Sometimes the decorations on Northwest Coast articles were so conventionalized that it is difficult to tell what they are. On the Tlingit shirt (right) there seems to be a killer whale; above, the design represents a thunderbird

odd, but out of these conventions as well as out of the realistic work, came by far the finest North American Indian art of historic times.

Perhaps the best known feature of the Northwest Coast is the totem pole. Totem poles were erected in the memory of a departed chief by his heirs, as part of the ceremony by which they publicly established their inheritance. The new chief thus honored his predecessor, and at the same time proclaimed his own importance. Poles marked the graves of chiefs, or actually were the graves, the body being placed inside. Poles were also erected to display some special privilege of the owner. Among some groups, a pole, with the door cut through it, was attached to the front of the house.

Events and triumphs, recent as well as ancient, could be recorded on totem poles. One, honoring a Haida chief, carried several figures of Russian priests. The chief had been very proud that he had successfully resisted the priests' attempts to convert him and his people. The figures represented that triumph and were a way of publicly ridiculing missionaries.

Model of a Haida house. The totem pole attached to the front, with the door cut through it, was quite common

Adze, the
Northwest carving
tool; this one is Kwakiutl

Another famous element of Northwest Coast culture was the function called the potlatch. Potlatches might be described as social ceremonials. They were gatherings at which a chief, with the help of his people, fed a great number of guests and either gave away or destroyed property. This was done by the chief to prove his own rank and privileges, or to confer certain crests, names, or rights on others, or both. When a chief died, his successor sometimes gave a potlatch or a series of potlatches in his memory. At these, the honors and powers he had inherited were recited, crests were displayed, ancestral contacts with divine animals were dramatically enacted. The guests served as witnesses that the new chief's claims were correct. The food and gifts they received were their payment, and the lavishness of the whole affair testified to the chief's high position and the position of his lineage group.

A potlatch was also sometimes given to announce an heir presumptive or, where inheritance was in the mother's line, to hand over certain crests and prerogatives to a son-in-law. The son-in-law would hold them as custodian for his children, to whom in due course he would pass them with another potlatch. Among some tribes, if a chief had suffered some humiliating accident, such as falling down in public, he might give a potlatch to restore his prestige. Among southern tribes, where the hereditary principle was weaker, potlatches were the means by which men in a sense "bought" the rank they desired.

At the potlatches, the crude but highly valued sheets of metal called "coppers" assumed their greatest importance. Among the northern tribes, it was essential that one or two of these coppers be destroyed at the first potlatch given by a dead chief's successor. This was done either by breaking them up and throwing them into the fire, or by throwing them into the sea. Farther south, coppers increased in value every time they were given away. Some of them became worth thousands of dollars.

There has been a great deal of disagreement about the extent of the "competitive potlatches" given with the hope of shaming or eliminating a rival. It seems likely that these occasionally occurred in early times, when there was a question of which of two chiefs ranked first. This situation could arise when two formerly independent villages united.

In the mid-nineteenth century, a number of Kwakiutl villages moved in around a Hudson's Bay post at Fort Rupert, and a number of Tsimshians similarly

Arriving in a ceremonial canoe, a party of visiting dignitaries prepares to embark at a Kwakiutl village for a potlatch. The highly decorated clothing and ornate headgear show the position and prestige of the participants; ordinarily few clothes were worn, but for special occasions, such as potlatches, everyone took pains to dress elegantly

Haida chief's ceremonial copper of the 1880's. It has the representation of a grizzly bear on its top

settled near a post at Port Simpson. Each of these gatherings formed loose confederacies. The ranking of the chiefs and nobles within each village was clear enough, but how they rated in regard to the chiefs of other units in their confederacy had never been worked out.

The result was a terrific competition. One chief would give a potlatch at, rather than for, a rival. His intent was to give away or destroy what he hoped was more wealth than the other could possibly amass. Blankets—both trade blankets and the far more valuable Chilkat ones—were burned, coppers were destroyed or had pieces hacked off them, and a slave or two was killed.

The second chief would call on his people, and they would make a tremendous effort to outdo the original potlatcher. Goods might be borrowed from outsiders, to be returned at a fixed rate of interest within a year —in itself no slight burden. Eventually one rival or the other would have to give up, and it would be established that he and his group were of lesser rank.

At its height, when the Indians were prospering mightily from the fur trade and their stock of material possessions was such as existed nowhere else in Indian North America, the competitive potlatch became

Greeting the incoming guests is a chief, carrying his staff of office. Above him, on the bank, another chief holds a ceremonial "copper." It will be given away and will become more valuable because of the transaction

Standing in front of a chief's house sometime around 1910, performers of the Southern Kwakiutl Shaman's Society pose for their picture. The figures wearing the huge bird masks represent a great man-eating bird of Kwakiutl mythology. The effect such performers had when conducting their spectacles indoors, by firelight, can be imagined

a vicious thing, an endless procedure of amassing wealth for the purpose of ruining others. Even so, the Indians sometimes managed to soften the business. Two chiefs who felt themselves called upon to assert themselves yet did not desire to be ruined or to come near to beggaring themselves and their people to win, would get together privately. They would agree to give a potlatch and a counterpotlatch at which the gifts and the things destroyed would come out exactly even. This gave the mass of the people an exciting show and resulted in no great damage.

The tribes at the north end of California were only part-way members of the Northwest Coast. Their potlatch was simplified, and did not include the giving away or destroying of wealth. Instead, thriftily, wealth was merely displayed. The most important items to the Californians were shell money and the skins of albino deer decorated with bands of brilliant, small feathers. Men of wealth hired dancers who, as the ceremony went on, progressively displayed more and more of these and other articles, including obsidian blades of great size manufactured only for show. Whoever displayed the most got the most glory, and

when the performance was over, the owners carefully retrieved all their goods.

The first well-established contact with the Northwest Coast Indians was made by Bering, the Dane for whom the Bering Straits are named, exploring for Russia. He sent ashore a boat which never returned. Instead, a number of war canoes came out against Bering's ship and he sailed away. In 1778, the great explorer Captain James Cook visited the Nootkas who gave him some sea otter skins. When members of the expedition reached China, Cook having died in the Hawaiian Islands, they discovered that the Chinese would pay tremendous prices for the furs. This was the beginning of the Northwest Coast trade which the Americans, especially, developed as a highly profitable triangular affair. Cheap goods were taken to the Northwest Coast to be traded for sea otter furs; the furs were traded at a high premium to the Chinese for tea, which was cheap in China; tea was sold in Boston at another high premium. The trade resulted in the virtual extinction of the sea otters, but while it lasted, everyone profited.

As the trade mounted, the Indians became choosy about the goods they would accept. An enterprising Yankee named Collins made a business of manufacturing, at Hartford, the kinds of knives, axes, and other blades that the Indians preferred. From this he branched into providing similar goods for natives in other parts of the world, with the result that to this day Collins and Company dominates the machete market of the world.

In the early nineteenth century the sea otter trade was replaced by trade in other furs, largely carried on through posts of such firms as the Hudson's Bay Company. The coastal Indians dealt in furs of their own taking, and in those they received in trade from Indians farther inland. They became rich in goods of all kinds, and through the middle of the nineteenth century they flourished.

Actual migration and settlement by white men came relatively late to the Northwest Coast. When it came, disease, liquor, and crowding had their usual effect. Slowly the culture faded, although as yet it is by no means dead. Commercial salmon fisheries and canneries took over many of the fishing grounds and for a time, until brought under government control, threatened the extermination of the salmon. Today the surviving tribes are getting along unevenly. Still men of the sea, they work for the fisheries and canneries when they are able. Some groups, with federal aid, have set up cooperatives with the hope of getting into the industry on their own. The tribes in Alaska are greatly handicapped by the fact that the non-Indians and commercial interests of the state have successfully prevented them from receiving reservations. They have title to little more than the sites of their villages, and such fishing grounds as they still control are always in danger of being seized by the powerful firms. Cut off from their subsidiary sources of livelihood, such as hunting, all too many try to live from salmon catch to salmon catch, spending much of the year in enforced, demoralizing idleness and struggling endlessly with accumulated debt.

In Oregon and Washington, fragments of many tribes, shattered by contact with large numbers of white men, have gathered on a few reservations under such circumstances as to destroy their original tribal distinctions. As a result they have lost a great part of their culture. Throughout the area nowadays, those who have dealings with tourists or who otherwise capitalize on their Indian heritage are likely to store away their ancient, meaningful insignia and put on war bonnets, that the white men may see what they intend to see.

To the Indians of northern California, the White Deerskin Dance took the place of the potlatch. Skins, such as the one shown above, were considered as valuable in California as Chilkat blankets were farther north. They were usually decorated with strands of brightly colored feathers. Below, Hupas perform a dance that was, in part, the ending of a long ritual with the purpose of "renewing the world" and assuring abundance. It was perhaps even more a means of displaying wealth, in particular the white deerskins and the large obsidian blades such as those that are carried by the two men in the front

The "button" and root of the peyote plant

Kiowa man's fan for use during a peyote ritual

Ghosts and Visions

The Paviotso prophet Jack Wilson, or Wovoka, who originated the Ghost Dance Cult, sketched in 1891

American Indian religions varied from the most primitive shamanism—little more than the exercise of magic, usually beneficial, by self-elected practitioners—to organized, priestly systems based on high philosophies. Whatever the type, one thing is constant: religion filled daily life. There was no such thing as setting aside a portion of every seventh day for relations with God or the gods.

For such people, when they saw the very framework of their lives collapsing, there was an inevitable turning to religion. In worship might be found the cure, or failure in worship might explain the creeping disaster that was destroying them, that was robbing life of all that made it worth living.

When primitive peoples are overwhelmed by a totally alien, higher culture, they have three choices. One is "nativism"—to reject the higher culture altogether and try to keep the old ways unchanged. In our modern age this seldom if ever works. The millions of men of the Machine Age press too remorselessly; also they offer too much that is useful and

Morning prayer in a peyote ceremony, interpreted by Tsa Toke, a Kiowa, who writes, "... he is under the potency of the peyote. The worshipper on both sides of the design shows them in meditation how their words they utter." Their prayers rise as birds. In the center are the fire, crescent-shaped altar, crossed eagle feather fans, and macaw feathers symbolizing morning

attractive. To take an extreme example, refusing to use metal tools would verge on insanity. For a generation or more, one tribe in the Southwest forbade its members to use a cultivator in their fields, insisting that its members stay "pure" by cultivating with hoes, which themselves were white men's products. Too many men came to realize how much horse-drawn cultivators could help them and lighten their work; in the end the ban was relaxed.

The second choice is complete acceptance of the higher culture, entirely abandoning the old one. This, also, seldom works. There are many individual exceptions, but usually the native who has cut himself off from all of his own tradition is an incomplete and uneasy man. There is too much learned in infancy— the warmth of certain types of family relationship, the satisfaction of familiar customs, a mode of thinking of one's self, a set of values—that nothing can satisfactorily replace. The Indians have a proud tradition; they are proud of their race and of their tribal history. They have a profound desire to continue to

be members of their tribe and to keep it in being. Given these things, you can begin to understand how some tribes remain still Indian after two or even three hundred years of contact with the white men, and after having been moved hundreds of miles from their original homes.

The third choice, and the most hopeful one, is making a new adaptation, taking what is good of the higher culture, keeping what is good of the older that can, as a practical matter, survive. In great degree this is what most Indians are trying to do. They have a hard time of it, not only because the white men habitually push them around, but even more because most white men hold the curious conviction that no people can become progressive unless it becomes *exactly* like themselves.

This explains why so many missionaries think that a man cannot become a good Christian unless he dresses as the missionary does, lives in the same kind of house, eats the same food—despite the fact that, as Indians sometimes point out, Our Lord wore His hair long and wrapped Himself in something that very closely resembled a blanket.

In terms of religion, the three choices could be somewhat inaccurately identified with three religious developments. The first is intended only to bring back the old days, such as the Ghost Dance Cult; the second, conversion to Christianity; the third, the modern, in-between, Peyote Cult or Native American Church. The identification is not exact. Such tribes as the Iroquois or the Zuñis of New Mexico show that an Indian can be "pagan" and progressive at the same time. Indians who hold strongly to tribe and tradition make excellent Christians, bringing to Christianity a sense of the constant presence of religion in daily life and a habit of participation in religious activities that we should do well to copy.

Nativistic or reactionary religious revivals and new sects appeared early after the white men grew strong on the continent. We have no report of any special religious development back of King Philip's des-

"Morning in Peyote Tepee." The worshippers purify themselves by fanning fragrant cedar smoke toward them. Above the tepee is Eagle Fan, on either side, Water Bird and Hawk. They all have symbolic meaning

A moment in an Arapaho Ghost Dance ritual. This picture is based on a photograph taken by James Mooney, a great, early ethnologist, who made an intensive study of the Ghost Dance

perate, futile counterattack in New England. Perhaps there was none, or perhaps the Puritans did not bother to record it. In the 1760's the Ottawa chief, Pontiac, nearly drove the British out of the Illinois-Ohio region. Back of Pontiac's success and the confederacy he formed were the preachings of a Delaware prophet, whose name is unknown. The prophet did not preach war, but a complete return to old ways, so that the good old days would return. Pontiac made the logical extension of this idea, that if the white men were cleared out, the good old days would come even faster.

Tecumseh's war against the Americans, in 1811 and 1812, was based on another revivalistic movement for return to the old, pure ways, led by his brother, Tenskwatawa, a rather unpleasant individual. The records on this man are ample. He had been an alcoholic who reformed after he had a shaman-type vision and proceeded to become a prophet. Like the forgotten Delaware, he did not preach war. He taught a return to purity, and in his doctrine the bringing back of old times, ample elbow room, and ample hunting were constant major elements; but he

did not teach a simple return to the old-time religion. Rather, he offered a new variant in which Christian influences are apparent. His doctrine also included such revolutionary novelties as ordering the destruction of sacred bundles.

The movement spread strongly among Indians who ranged from uneasy to desperate. Tecumseh, the man of action, the war leader, seized upon it as the source of the necessary emotional element for his war.

The influence of Christianity shows in many of the cults, sects, and religions that sprang up among the Indians. The concept of a single, active, high God has been hit upon only a few times in human history. When that concept was brought to the Indians, there were plenty of competent religious thinkers who, although they rejected the new religion, were strongly influenced by this fundamental element of it. It resulted in giving a new coherence to old systems, and to the development of new variants.

After the Revolution, the Iroquois were a defeated people, their power gone, their empire cut down to reservations. They, too, felt hopelessness, frustration, and the sad sense of the dying away of the old, rich

189

life. Among them in 1799 arose a prophet, Handsome Lake. He, too, was an alcoholic who reformed after a vision. He preached that the old Iroquois had had a good life, but that it was incomplete because they knew God incompletely. His new dispensation made the old religion complete. He combined established, old ceremonies with new ones. Originally he taught an extreme reaction against white ways but later he modified his stand, even to the extent of agreeing to the use of ploughs. This was a more important change than it seems at first look, because ploughing is a man's activity. The introduction of plough farming ended the women's monopoly and affected their whole position. Handsome Lake's ministry did not result in any fighting. It helped the Iroquois to survive and to fight the plague of drunkenness, and it gave their religion a form that could survive strongly to the present day.

Far more famous than any of these early religious revivals is the Ghost Dance Cult. Its history is curious. it is directly the result of Christian mission influence,

and it started, of all places, among the Paviotso, a branch of the Pah-Utes, in Nevada. There, about 1888, an Indian with a history of mission contacts, Jack Wilson or Wovoka, began having visions. The visions produced a doctrine that was in part derived from an older relative of similar background, Tavibo, probably an uncle, who had some visions and took a try at being a prophet in 1870. The new religion combined Christian ethical ideas and the general idea of a messiah to come, with rituals intended to make the white men disappear and bring back the vanished game and the dead Indians. Wovoka specifically preached peace and forbade his converts from engaging in warfare or fighting anyone.

Word of this teaching reached the Plains tribes when things were desperate. The buffalo were gone, and everyone was hungry to the verge of starvation. All the tribes had been defeated and put on reservations. Life was wretched, and they did not know what way to turn. Delegations went to talk to the prophet. The warlike Plains tribes soon made an important

Composite painting of an Arapaho Ghost Dance made from photographs taken by James Mooney. The Basin-type "round dance" with women participating was new to the Plains

190

The climax of the Ghost Dance—two women, in an entranced state, having visions

change in his teachings. War against the whites was an essential part of their Ghost Dance doctrine. Dancing in a circle, Basin style, would bring back the dead buffalo and their own dead tribesmen; but it was their own power, magically fortified, that would clear their land of the great enemy. Through the rituals and by use of various symbols that developed around it, they could make themselves bulletproof, or endow a shirt with the magical property of turning bullets.

Some of the Sioux, the Arapahos, Cheyennes, and Kiowas accepted the doctrine most completely. It led to a strange ferment, endless dancing, and the announcement of many visions in which people saw the buffalo, talked with the returning dead, prophesied the new millennium. There were sporadic acts of hostility. The white men became badly frightened. The situation led to the killing of Sitting Bull and to Wounded Knee, the last battle between Plains Indians and soldiers, described on page 142. After that the cult died away. It is forgotten now, except that some Nevada Indians still perform dances in a form Wovoka established.

None of these religions lasted except the Handsome Lake dispensation, and that never spread beyond the Iroquois. What is powerful today is the most curious of all—the Peyote Cult. Peyote (pronounced pay-YO-tee) is a small, spineless cactus of which only a very small piece, the "button," shows above ground. This button may be chewed or steeped to make a tea. It contains a number of alkaloids which cause the taker to have visions, usually of great beauty, in which he seems to be in communication with divinity. The causing of visions fits in neatly with the vision complex of the Plains Indians and their neighbors. Definitely not habit-forming, the plant does not come under the control of the Federal Narcotics Act.

Before they had peyote, a number of tribes in the United States used the mescal bean to cause somewhat similar effects. Many people confuse the two plants. They are not related in any way.

Peyote had long been used ceremonially by certain Mexican tribes. Perhaps as early as the seventeenth century it spread to the Tonkawas and Karankawas of Texas, reached the Kiowas and Comanches in Oklahoma in the 1870's, and about ten years later began spreading widely west of the Mississippi.

With it went the "Peyote Cult," a religion compounded from original Mexican elements and many later additions. Ceremonies are usually held in a tepee. They begin at nightfall and end with a feast

191

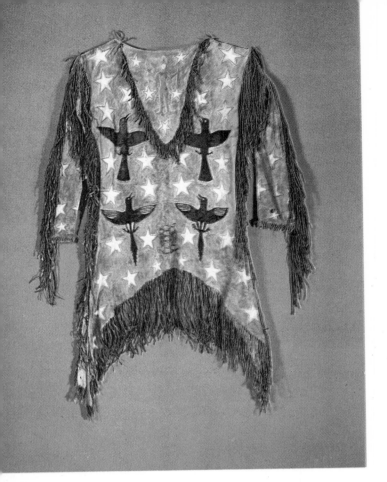

in the morning. Participants describe their feelings at that time as peacefulness, happiness, and a sense of being blessed. People whose lives have become dreary and aimless find in peyote worship and its visions a means of transcending the sad realities and the bleakness about them.

The rituals and beliefs may be purely Indian or contain Christian elements. At the center, always, is the plant itself, which is regarded as sacred and the consumption of which is in part a form of communion.

As peyote does not grow much north of the Mexican border, in many places it is hard to get and often scarce. When there is, say, only a single button for a sizable congregation, it may simply be displayed on the primitive altar, without anyone eating it. The actual eating is accompanied by solemn ritual. The variation in belief is exemplified by the idea held in one tribe that the staff used by the leader of the ritual is "the staff of life," while another tribe holds that the staff is Christ's.

The use of peyote has spread throughout the many tribes now gathered in Oklahoma. It has also spread northwards across the Canadian border, among Plains, Woodlands, and Western Farmer tribes, has reached into Oregon, and in the last few years has made great progress among the Navahos. Those

Oglala Sioux Ghost Dance by Frederic Remington. With the buffalo gone and the white men surrounding them and hemming them in, the Sioux took readily to the Ghost Dance in hopes of bringing back the old days

A peyote ritual in a tepee, painted about 1910 by Ernest Spybuck, a Kickapoo

who take up the cult often abandon their old religions, although some merge the two, and are usually immune to conversion to Christianity. They become members of a new, intertribal religion, the sharing of which gives them a sense of belonging to something larger, less helpless, than their own small group.

Because of its effect upon the old religions and Christianity, no Indian manifestation of recent years has aroused such violent controversy. The controversy is made more violent and more confused by the fear most people feel toward "taking a drug," although many careful experiments have proven that this is no drug. Opponents make statements ranging from one that peyote causes bad teeth to allegations of fantastic orgies and the utter ruination of those who use the plant. Peyotists state, apparently with considerable truth, that members of their cult do not drink and usually are quiet, steady citizens. Many hold that the plant will cure sicknesses, which is a dangerous belief.

In order to meet the attacks upon the cult, especially drives to forbid by law the possession or use

of the plant, many of the peyotists have organized themselves into the Native American Church, a formal, nonprofit corporation. The very fact that this "Indianistic" movement can do so modern a thing is an interesting example of the third choice mentioned earlier in this chapter—making a new adaptation out of parts of the old and parts of the new.

There are indications that the cult is weakening in some of the places where it first grew to strength, even while it spreads to new tribes. What its future will be, no one can tell.

Among some of the Indians of the Northwest, on the coast and farther inland, there exists a curious derivative from the extinct Shaker sect of Christianity. Apparently the Shaker pattern of getting up and dancing and prophesying under sudden inspiration fits the old shamanistic pattern of inspiration. At present this Indian shakerism cannot be classified as Christian, despite the fact that it contains some strong Christian elements. Whatever it is now, however, the indications are that this group will end up as an odd Christian sect.

193

Modern basket of the Passamaquoddys

The Non-Vanishing Americans

Modern tribal self-government—Navahos voting in a tribal election on their reservation. A special system of ballots on which the pictures of the candidates are printed is used, since most Navahos do not know how to read

Anything like a complete description of the Indians of the United States as they are today would require all of a book the size of this one. It is as true of them now as it was before the white men came that there is hardly a general statement that can be made about Indians that does not call for a long list of exceptions.

One big fact stands out: The Indians are not vanishing; they are increasing. It is probable that the "federal" Indian population dropped as low as 300,000 around the turn of the century. Today there are about 450,000 "federal" Indians in the United States, including the Aleuts and Eskimos in Alaska. These are people who are recognized as Indians by federal law, and have the protections and rights and are subject to the restrictions that come with that recognition.

In addition to the federal Indians, there are remnants of tribes that have no federal status. Some, like the Passamaquoddys and Micmacs of Maine and the Pamunkeys of Virginia, are recognized by the states in which they live and have land set aside for their use. Many others are recognized only to the extent that, in most of the South, they are segregated and that, although many of them are partly or mostly of

San Carlos Apache cattlemen drive their herd across a stream on the reservation. The tribe built up their herd of white-faced cattle from a motley collection of "pink and green" creatures, and only did so over the strong protests of white cattle interests

white descent, it is unlawful, in the states where they live, for whites to marry them. On the whole they are scattered, depressed people, poor farmers, who have lost virtually all of their old traditions and tribal organizations. Many of them have tried at different times to gain federal recognition and be placed under the jurisdiction of the Bureau of Indian Affairs, but without success. Where there are no segregating laws, such groups, like the New England Indians who were not moved west, tend to disappear. They become white men who claim an Indian ancestor somewhere in their family tree.

To find recognizable Indians who retain something of tribal organization and of Indian life, you must look to the groups that have the status of Indians under federal law. These range from the 10,000-odd Iroquois in New York State to the strong tribes of the Southwest. The greatest centers of Indian population are in Oklahoma with more than 110,000, Arizona with an estimated 75,000, and New Mexico and Alaska with about 50,000 each. The tribes of Arizona, New Mexico, and Alaska are native to those states; most of those in Oklahoma were moved there

Anna Wauneka, one of the most forceful and modern of Navaho leaders, always dresses in traditional style

Sioux girls arrive at the government's Carlisle Indian School, 1879, to be "de-Indianized." Their expressions indicate how they feel about this prospect

under the old policy of concentrating as many tribes as possible in "Indian Territory."

In the north, in the two Dakotas and adjacent states, there are some 20,000 Sioux. The scattered groups of Indians in California add up to over 17,000, and Indians in considerable numbers are to be found in Oregon, Washington, Nevada, Idaho, Montana, Wisconsin, and Minnesota.

In previous chapters there have been brief descriptions of the later history of the various groups. The story always seems to be monotonously and sadly the same. There are three types of tribal history. Some tribes, especially in the East, were wiped out. Many were forcibly moved out of the white man's way, sometimes several times, until finally they landed in some unlikely spot where they have been allowed to remain. Others, especially the stronger Western and Southwestern tribes, have been allowed to keep some part of their original homeland.

Until the 1870's we dealt with the tribes as little nations having a limited sovereignty subordinate to our own, making regular treaties with them each time

we wanted a new arrangement. Finally Congress stopped the treaty-making, and since then we have dealt with the Indians somewhat more honestly as people under our jurisdiction, even though we did not recognize most of them as citizens until 1924.

Whether we had treaties with them or only made agreements and promises, it is an unhappy truth that there is no tribe with which we have not at some time broken our word.

When gold was found in the country of the progressive Cherokees, who were moving so rapidly toward full civilization, we drove them out. Since at that time the non-Indian population of the South was increasing rapidly and wanted all the rich land it could get, while we were at it, we drove out all of the Five Civilized Tribes that we could catch.

The story changes somewhat as we move westward and forward to more recent times. When gold was found in the sacred Black Hills of the Sioux, the government tried to make our citizens respect the Sioux boundaries, but could not stop the rush. In the end, the Indians were stripped of a large portion of their land, but they were not driven entirely out of their own country. The national conscience had become more awake, and furthermore, there was objection to the expense of Indian wars.

The happy reverse of the Cherokee and Sioux stories can be seen in events on the Navaho reservation since 1920, when oil was first discovered there, followed later by helium, then uranium and other valuable minerals, and by yet more, vast deposits of oil. The government has scrupulously protected the rights of the tribe. Following the law, leases are let by open bidding and must be approved by both the tribal council and the Secretary of the Interior.

The number of educated Navahos is still woefully small, although it is increasing. The tribe now has, not an attorney, but a staff of attorneys. Well aware of its rights, it grants no leases or permits to prospect without the best possible terms. Some of the bidders grumble, some are really hurt that they should have to make to a bunch of ignorant Indians the same concessions they would have to make to a corporation of white men, but they meet the terms. The income that the tribe has received so far has not been enough to

relieve the desperate poverty of many of its members, but it has enabled the tribe to undertake the remarkable program of self-help mentioned earlier.

The modern Indian picture contains all sorts of curiosities. A very few tribes—such as the Osages and, in the last several years, the Jicarilla Apaches—receive a considerable income from oil and similar leases. With the sudden acquisition of money, following poverty and deprivation, has come an unfortunate amount of debauchery. Oil-rich Indians, however, are very few, nor are most of these as rich as popular belief makes out. An Osage with as much as $1,000 a year in oil money is above average.

The Iroquois were strong enough to receive reservations in their own country in New York, where about ten thousand of them remain to this day. Mostly mixed in blood, they are still proudly Iroquois. A generation or so ago, a bridge was built across the Saint Lawrence River, one end of it being on the reservation occupied by the Mohawks. Indians got jobs as common laborers. Much interested in what was going on, they showed remarkable ability in climbing all over the structure, an apparently inborn

Masked Senecas go from house to house during the spring house purification ceremony at Coldspring on the Allegany Reservation in New York State, April 12, 1941

A Mohawk high steel worker positions a beam high on a building going up on lower Manhattan. Mohawks began going into this kind of work in 1886, when a bridge was built across the Saint Lawrence River, close to their reservation. Their catlike agility and their lack of fear of heights make them ideal for this specialized kind of work

surefootedness, and a lack of fear of heights. Presently some of them were promoted to steelworking jobs; in the end there were Mohawk riveters.

Interest in this type of work spread among the tribes of the League. Today, structural steel work, and especially work on the "high iron" of skyscrapers and great bridges, is an Iroquois specialty. Iroquois, both Christians and the followers of Handsome Lake's revision of the ancient faith, have worked on most of the important steel structures in the country, clear across to the Golden Gate Bridge. Because New York City provides a great deal of such work and the Brooklyn Navy Yard is a source of steady employment, there is an Iroquois colony in Brooklyn. The Christians attend a church with a minister who preaches in Mohawk, the "pagans" hold simple ceremonies in their apartments, and all go home at intervals to maintain contact with their tribe.

In this chapter there have been references to "federal" Indians, and throughout the book there have been references to reservations. It is time to explain the somewhat complicated question of what a reservation is and what the status of an Indian is. In both there have been changes.

Reservations originally were areas of land reserved for Indians, to which they were supposed to be confined. The idea of confinement has long been forgotten. A reservation today is a tract of land, large or small, good or worthless, reserved for the exclusive use of a specific group of Indians and held in trust for that group by the United States. It is exempt from taxation, and so is income derived from it. No part of it can be sold, given away, taken by foreclosure or other process, rented or leased without the consent of both the owners and the trustee. The trustee in important matters is the Secretary of the Interior, in minor ones the Commissioner of Indian Affairs. The government is also responsible for ensuring that the land is properly used and its resources not wasted. One tribe, owning a valuable stand of timber, talked the trustee into agreeing to a sale of the timber that resulted in great waste and damage and a poor return to the tribe. When the Indians woke up to what they had let themselves in for, they successfully sued the United States for several million dollars of compensation since the trustee had failed in his duty!

Such land is called "trust land," because it is in trust, and "restricted land," since its owners are restricted to some extent in their use of it, more so in disposing of it. Granted the restriction, the ownership of such land, tax exempt and producing tax-

Two Navaho leaders: Bullet (later Manuelito) in 1868 and 1874, and Chee Dodge in 1930

exempt income, is obviously a desirable thing; any of us might like to enjoy the same right.

A reservation has another important quality. In legal language, it is "Indian country." With certain special exceptions, Indian country is exempt from state law, and state courts and police have no authority within it. It is subject to federal law, lawsuits arising within it are tried in federal courts, major crimes are controlled by federal statutes. For the Indians within Indian country, lesser crimes, including some that rate as felonies, and such matters as marriage, divorce, and ordinary business relationships are under the jurisdiction of the tribe. This jurisdiction is the foundation on which tribal self-government, even the continued existence of tribes as tribes, exists. All strong tribes maintain their own police and courts, and jealously guard their right of home rule.

An Indian may leave his reservation any time he likes, without asking anyone's permission (except for a couple of pueblos in the Southwest, which still enforce their old law requiring permission from their own government before a tribesman can absent himself). He can come back whenever he chooses. It can clearly be seen that reservations are *not* "concentration camps," despite much hysterical talk and even some hysterical books to the contrary.

Joint Indian-federal jurisdiction over Indian country goes back to the beginnings of our legal history and has been upheld over and over again by the

Paul Jones, present head of the Navaho Tribal Council

Supreme Court. It is an expression of their ancient, limited sovereignty. Congress can terminate it at will, and many times the Indians have been greatly afraid that Congress would do so.

Why do the Indians fear the state jurisdiction that the rest of us take for granted? Why are they so anxious to stay exempt from what one writer has called "the tender mercies of state sovereignty"? The answer is no credit to us. In the states with Indian populations can be found individuals and groups, even local organizations, sincerely friendly to Indians

199

A meeting of the Navaho Tribal Council. Under the leadership of a series of able chairmen, starting with the late Chee Dodge, the Council has become an effective governing body

and working for their welfare and advancement. Yet it is true today as it has been true throughout our history that those who adjoin Indian country are those who discriminate most strongly against Indians.

The hostile attitude, the belief that Indians are shiftless and worthless make it difficult or impossible for Indians to compete with non-Indians for jobs. They are used as a justification for trying to separate Indians from their property—above all, as always, from their land. If today it cannot be used to separate Indians from their land, it can be used to prevent them from exploiting it, thus enabling white men to get the use of it cheap.

For instance: Parts of several Apache tribes were settled on the San Carlos Reservation in Arizona, where for many years they sickened in idleness and survived on government rations. The reservation embraced a lot of good grazing land. Neighboring cattlemen argued that Apaches never could or would

use that range; white men should have it. Under duress, under the eternal threat of troops, the Apaches signed away about a quarter of the reservation.

All the good remainder was leased to a few powerful cattle companies. When, with the guidance and encouragement of a fine superintendent, in the early 1920's, the Apaches started running some small bunches of cattle of hopelessly mixed breed on the most worthless parts, the cattlemen were only amused. Then, by the most intense efforts, the Apache cattlemen began making a little money and buying good bulls, so that their herds were working up to where they were presentable, salable beef cattle. With the superintendent's support, the tribe refused to renew certain leases, needing the range to expand the Indians' own operations. Immediately the pressure became heavy upon senators and congressmen and upon the Indian Bureau, with outraged demands for the superintendent's removal.

The senators from Arizona showed conscience, the Indian Bureau was firm. There was a·good deal of backing and filling, but by 1932 there were some 28,000 head of Indian-owned cattle grazing the range and all the leases had been ended. Still, the cattle interests had a string tied to it, for the Apaches were not allowed to breed their own bulls.

Their herds had started with odd longhorns, dairy cows, anything they could get their hands on. To get decent beef cattle required careful breeding with registered bulls and continuous culling of off-colored cows. To produce suitable bulls, you must have a bull-breeding herd of registered cows and registered bulls. Otherwise you must be continuously buying expensive bulls from other breeders. As the big Apache operation grew prosperous, the Indian cattlemen were required to spend thousands of dollars of their profits yearly buying good sires from non-Indians. Registered heifers they could not buy.

Under the same superintendent, a man no one could frighten, they solved their problem during the great drought of the 1930's. In this they had the cooperation (some non-Indian cattlemen would say the connivance) of the Commissioner of Indian Affairs. As a relief measure, the government was buying cattle from drought-devastated ranches. Some "drought relief cattle" were issued to Indians, many were butchered and distributed as food for relief purposes. The superintendent spotted a herd of registered heifers that was due to be bought before the creatures starved to death. The heifers were quietly shipped to the San Carlos Reservation. They were in such miserable condition that nobody thought twice about them. On the Apache grass they prospered, and suddenly the cattle interests were presented with something done and finished—the Indians had a registered bull-breeding herd. The fuss is all over now, the situation is taken for granted, and in the last few years the San Carlos cattlemen have begun *selling registered bulls to white men.*

Until recently, too, these Indians were plagued by a petty war of attrition—fences cut, cattle "strayed," calves mavericked—an endless small harassment and thievery. It was difficult to cope with, since the missing animals had been driven outside Indian country, where state law prevailed. The San Carlos Reservation lies in two counties. The situation has improved

vastly since 1950, when the Apaches made it very plain that they would vote for those county officials, especially sheriffs, who gave them equal treatment. It is remarkable how a solid bloc of several hundred votes can reduce a man's race prejudice.

This is only one example, and it happens to be one with a happy ending. Others, many with quite different endings, can be found wherever there are Indians. In towns near reservations, Indians are often Jim-Crowed. They are abused by the police, get the book thrown at them in local courts, are exploited for their money and contemptuously rejected for other purposes. This is no universal picture, but all too widely true. California, Minnesota, Wisconsin, and New York have shown real conscience toward their Indians; other states, such as New Mexico, seem to be waking up. Yet New York, by a fancy bit of legal interpreting, prevents Iroquois parents from voting in the school elections, although their children are in the state schools. In the last ten years, in New Mexico, Nebraska, and South Dakota, white men have murdered Indians and either have not been charged or have received a suspended sentence.

Here is one example: In a Nebraska town, near one of the Sioux reservations over the border in South Dakota, a white man looking out his window saw a Sioux named Standing Bear, against whom he had a grudge, coming down the street. He seized a baseball bat, ran out, and beat Standing Bear over the head with it until the Indian fell unconscious. Police picked Standing Bear up and threw him in jail, where he died in a few hours. The white man was arrested, pleaded guilty to manslaughter, and got a two years' suspended sentence. This, please note, is only one

Tribal court of the Shoshone-Bannocks in Idaho. A woman has here been accused of assault; being the sole support of her children, she was not confined but sentenced instead to wash the Agency windows each week

example: it could be multiplied many times. From the Indians' point of view, the rub is that had this crime been committed in Indian country, the defendant would have come up in federal court and would have got his just deserts, which leads to the even bigger point that had the white man encountered Standing Bear in Indian country, he would not have dared kill him.

This is why Indians with few exceptions hold strongly to their ancient right of home rule and federal protection, and why, for all their constant dissatisfactions with the Bureau of Indian Affairs, they prefer its jurisdiction to that of the states. It also explains their great alarm and sense of betrayal when in 1953 there was enacted, over strong Indian protest, a law giving any state the right to take jurisdiction over Indian country any time it so wishes. The Indians and their friends have been struggling ever since to get rid of this law.

Indians have certain special rights as Indians, other than their jurisdiction over their land and exemption of that land from taxes. Their education, health service, and a number of other services that most of us get from counties or states are federal responsibilities so long as the Indians reside on their reservations. When an Indian moves off the reservation he is on the same footing as anybody else, although in practice most federal Indian schools and hospitals receive nonreservation Indians. The use of special, segregated, federal schools for Indians is decreasing; and in seventeen states many, and in some states all, the Indians go to the state public schools, with which the government makes contracts.

Indians do not get pensions from the government. Uncle Sam does not feed them. One of the many frustrations Indians encounter when they go to the cities seeking work is that employers, and also people concerned with relief, if the Indian winds up out of luck, will say, "Why don't you go back to the reservation and let the government take care of you?" The government won't take care of him. Indian rights to relief are the same as anyone else's, less what some states refuse to give. Occasionally, in extreme cases, when some disaster has a whole community starving, the Indian Bureau will manage to finagle some surplus commodities out of the Department of Agriculture and sometimes a little money from Congress, but these are exceptions.

Leaving aside a few alcoholics at one end and a small number of old die-hards at the other, Indians want to progress. They want to progress *as Indians*. They see no reason why they cannot be Indians—even more, Apaches or Cheyennes or Iroquois or Sioux—and at the same time be entirely competent in our modern world. The feeling that it has been made impossible for them thus to win back to a good life without losing their identities is a principal cause of the heavy drinking now so common among them.

By and large Indians are poor. They range from poor to horribly poor. They are, when they wish to be, extremely picturesque, and they are objects of great interest to tourists. For this reason, a great many Indians are in the tourist business. That they show themselves off, perform parts of old ceremonies for gain, and peddle their wares, does not mean that they are frauds or have lost their dignity. It means only that they like eating regularly as much as we do.

For the same reasons, a number of Indians have made their way to Hollywood and others pick up some badly needed cash at times when motion picture companies come out their way on location, even though often they know that how they are dressed and what they are told to do is ridiculous. As a matter of fact, a source of constant anger to Indians is the way they are represented in the majority of movies. Above all they are sick of the eternally repeated lie that makes them out as savage aggressors against innocent whites.

Navaho jewelry left in the trading post as security, to be redeemed by money received when lambs are sold. The owners often borrow their possessions back for a day or so, to take part in one of the ceremonies or dances

A shanty on the Oklahoma Cherokee reservation. Poverty and overcrowding in such homes invite disease

A Sioux dwelling on the Pine Ridge reservation—the standard type of home for these 20th century Americans

Present-day San Ildefonso. Except for the modern automobiles, few changes have been made. Children play in the dust beneath a tree, and the houses form a single, long block just like the houses of the early Pueblo people as shown on pages 10—11

The tourists come with many preconceived notions. An Indian in a business suit disappoints them. Some years ago a visiting newspaperman went to see the Corn Dance, a major ceremony, at the Pueblo of Cochiti, New Mexico. He concluded that the thing was a fraud because the supervisor of the dance was a young man with a crew haircut who worked at a white-collar job in the atomic center of Los Alamos. The newspaperman published a foolish article to this effect. He was too blind to see the truth, which was that the ceremony was so genuine and the belief so deep that this very modern young man would take several days' leave of absence to perform his part in it. Many Indians throughout the country, learning what tourists expect, make efforts to give it to them.

Interior at San Ildefonso. The decorations above the windows, the fireplace, and the ceremonial garments hanging from a pole all go back thousands of years

Mescalero woman and child. Buckskin dresses painted yellow were typical of Southern and Mescalero Apaches

They don war bonnets and imitations of Plains leggings and do other things that are little more than theatricals. In quiet, they laugh their heads off and make fun of the tourists and of themselves.

A good many tribes, as a result of all the jostling and shoving around and hardship to which they have been subjected, have lost the externals of their old cultures, forgotten their rituals, forgotten their way of dressing. At present a synthetic, pan-Indian culture is spreading among such tribes, largely based on Plains costume and Plains modes of dancing. They take it up because they crave a means of asserting that they are still Indian.

Again with some exceptions, Indian family ties are deep and strong, and Indians are passionately fond of children and delightful with them. Indian children are well brought up, but in most tribes they are never struck. The family feeling reaches wide, to grandparents, brothers and sisters, cousins, uncles, aunts, children, nieces, and nephews. It is unthinkable to abandon them or refuse them help. From this arises one of the serious problems of the Indian who goes

Modern Deer Dance at Santa Clara Pueblo, New Mexico. The dancers represent both the deer and the hunters. The costume is ancient, except that white, commercial shirts have replaced coarse, cotton shirts of native weave. The drummer is wearing modern Western clothes

A Flathead Indian in Montana operates the band-saw sharpener belonging to his family's lumber company

Skilled workers in a Phoenix plant. The man farthest back is white, the other three Indian, tribe unspecified

to the city to earn his living. In his family are old people, children, perhaps a sick or crippled relative, going hungry at home. He supports them. If they follow him, he takes them in. Even if he has worked himself up into semiskilled or skilled employment, the load is so heavy that you could say he shares his relatives' poverty, rather than that they share his comparative wealth.

An Indian seeking employment has a tough time. Thin-skinned, proud, shy, and thoroughly uneasy in his new situation, he is readily discouraged, and usually appears stupid and unable to talk. Until employers have had experience with Indians, they are likely to be prejudiced against them. The foreman's way of giving orders may be normal to us, but shockingly insulting by Indian standards. The idea of absolute regularity, of turning up *every* day, at the *same* hour, has to be learned. Once Indians have got past all these hurdles and learned how the system works, they do very well, and are particularly desired in jobs requiring fine manual skill.

So there they are, nearly half a million of them. They have a tough struggle, and it is no wonder that many get discouraged, yet they refuse to give up. One of the amazing things about them is their loyalty to the United States. No Communist has ever been able to get to first base with them. Their record in World War I, World War II, and the Korean War is magnificent, not only in the armed forces, but in the way that, out of their poverty, they scrimped and scraped to give to the Red Cross, buy war bonds, help in every way they could. Many Indians, registering for the draft, turned up with their rifles, ready to go.

The Iroquois made a fuss about being drafted. In World War I, Indians were exempt, so the League of the Iroquois passed its own draft act and sent its young men into the National Guard. They took it as an insult to be called up under compulsion.

Florida Seminoles on the reservation at Dania, hollowing a dugout canoe. The men at work wear the typical Seminole shirts; the man watching (right) wears an older style costume. The house is in the traditional style

Maria Martinez, most famous of all modern Indian potters, and her late husband, Julian, polishing pots preparatory to painting the designs on them. The pottery revival sparked by this remarkable couple worked wonders for San Ildefonso, where poverty had been intense

A fine example of moden Indian crafts—a basket with a knobbed lid, made by Mrs. Kickax of the Karok tribe of California, one of the most famous of modern Indian basket makers. At right, a Navaho woman at her loom

207

Early 20th century Seneca mask

An example of the pottery style of Lucy Lewis of Acoma Pueblo, with designs taken from primitive specimens

Corn Dance at Cochiti by Quah Ah, the first outstanding Pueblo woman painter. Chorus and orchestra are at right

"Koshare of Taos" by Pablita Velarde of Santa Clara Pueblo. The Taos sacred clowns make a mixture of comedy and ritual out of climbing the pole for the food at the top during the annual Saint Jerome's Day festival. If they fail to climb the pole, it is an extremely bad omen

Modern Iroquois wood carving of an Iroquois-style tug-of-war. Sometimes the participants sit for the contest

"Navaho Weaver" by Tsinnahjinnie, a highly gifted Navaho artist. Coming from one of the most primitive sections of the reservation, he began copying Pueblo artists at school in Santa Fe. He has since established his own style, and has influenced later Navaho artists

The brighter side of Navaho life—the fair arrives on the reservation. In spite of their intense, dispiriting poverty, these people, like all of us, find much to enjoy in life

The veterans are home now, and all the Indians are struggling. They want and need help to help themselves, and they are worried and angry because government policy so often seems to deny them the opportunity to do so. Instead, it has made credit harder to get, weakened a number of tribal enterprises, tried to override tribal councils or even displace them, and has encouraged the loss of desperately needed land. Worse, there is always present a strong trend towards what is called "termination," which is a means of getting rid of the Indian problem by passing laws declaring, in effect, that certain tribes are no longer Indians, their reservations are to be broken up, their governments dissolved, their rights as Indians ended. Plans laboriously worked out between various tribes and the local Indian Service employees for workable programs of rehabilitation too often lie gathering dust. Termination frightens the tribes even worse than does the threat of state jurisdiction.

The picture is dreary, but still these remarkable people can drum and sing, joke and laugh—even if some of the jokes are bitter. They have not given up. They do not want handouts or charity; they want the guidance and help that is necessary to enable them to help themselves. With a little understanding from their fellow Americans, they still may attain their goal, which is to be as healthy, as competent in all our ways, as active contributors, as solidly self-supporting as the rest of us, and still hold to traditions, generosities, and ancient knowledge that will add greatly to the richness of the American scene.

210

School's out at Santa Ana Pueblo, New Mexico. There must be hope and a future for youngsters like these

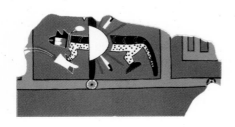

INDEX

(Italicized page numbers refer to illustrations.)

BELLA BELLA BELLA COOLA SARSI B L A C K F E E T W E S T E R N

KWAKIUTL CHILCOTIN SHUSWAP BLOOD GROS VENTRE

COMOX LILLOOET PIEGAN ARAPAHO N. D.

NOOTKA COWICHAN OKINAGAN THOMPSON KUTENAI C R O W HIDATSA TETO DAKOTA

MAKAH LUMMI METHOW KALISPEL WASH. MANDAN S. D.

QUILEUTE SKAGIT SALISH SPOKAN PEND TUNAHE MONT. ARIKARA SUTAIO

QUINAIELT CHEMAKUM COEUR D'OREILLES K I O W A APACHE SUTAIO

CHEHALIS TWANA NISQUALLI D'ALENE PALOUSE OMA

KWALHIOQUA CHINOOK COWLITZ NEZ FLATHEAD PONCA

TILLAMOOK WASCO PERCES CAYUSE C O M A N C H E NEB.

YAQUINA KALAPOOIA MOLALA ORE. UMATILLA IDAHO H I G H PAWNEE

ALSEA UMPQUA YAKIMA BANNOCK KAN

SIUSLAW TAKELMA KLIKITAT W Y O. W E S

COOS TUTUTNI KLAMATH SHOSHONE COLO. KANS.

TOLOWA MODOC G R E A T PADUCAH

YUROK SHASTA PAVIOTSO B A S I N UTE APACHE

WIYUT KAROK HUPA GOSIUTE P L A I N S

WAILAKI ACHOMAWI NEV. JICARILLA OKLA.

MATTOLE YANA ATSUGEWI WASHO UTE N A V A H O APACHE WICHITA

KATO WINTUN MONO UTAH TANOAN KERES

YUKI MAIDU C A L I F O R N I A WALAPAI HOPI N. M. TAWAKON

POMO MIWOK YOKUTS YAVAPAI ZUÑI

WAPPO KERN CALIF. COYOTERO MESCALERO KIC

COSTANOAN RIVER CHEMEHUEVI MOHAVE ARIZ. APACHE TEXAS TO

SALINAN CHUMASHAN CAHUILLA MARICOPA PIMA MIMBREÑO APACHE

SERRANO GABRIELEÑO LUISEÑO DIEGUEÑO YUMA PAPAGO APACHE

LAGUNA COCOPA S O U T H W E S T Rio Grande LIPAN APACHE

Cochimi Seri Opata Rio Grande

Nevome Tarahumare Concho Toboso

Yaqui Coahuilteco

Mayo

Acaxee Tepehuane

Nahuatl Zacateco Pame

Waicuri Cora Huichol Tamaulipeco

N O R T H W E S T   C O A S T

P L A T E A U

S O U T H W E S T